CLASSIC CARS

SINCE 1945

photography
Jasper Spencer-Smith

CLASSIC CARS

SINCE 1945

MICHAEL TWITE

BLANDFORD PRESS

Poole   Dorset

First published in the U.K. 1981 by
Blandford Press
Link House, West Street,
Poole, Dorset BH15 1LL
Copyright © 1981 Blandford Books Ltd

ISBN 0 7137 1065 9

Filmset by Keyspools Ltd, Golborne, Lancs, U.K.
Printed in Singapore

CONTENTS

HKY 547

INTRODUCTION

B ritish and American car collectors have a fetish for classifying their machines into particular groups. Over the years a bewildering number of categories have evolved, not necessarily to define what belongs to a particular group, but very often to decide what is unacceptable.

In Britain the Veteran Car Club caters only for cars built until the end of 1904, and only cars built before 1905 are eligible for the London to Brighton Veteran Car Run, which happens every November. And it is unwise to call them 'old crocks' within the earshot of a member of the Veteran Car Club!

In 1934 a group of car enthusiasts got together and decided to form a club. catering for older sports cars. This was originally to be called the Veteran Sports Car Club, but in deference to the Veteran Car Club they eventually hit on the title of the Vintage Sports Car Club. They rather arbitrarily decided that no car built after the end of 1930 would be eligible for the club, on the basis that mass production and the use of unit construction chassis/body units was removing individuality from the motor car. They also felt that the depression years of 1929 and 1930 marked the end of many famous manufacturers and therefore the end of most fine motor cars.

The club decided to sub-divide their cars further, calling the cars made between 1905 and 1916 'Edwardians', leaving the 'vintage' period to run from 1919 to 1930. Since there was very little production during World War I this was a convenient enough date.

As the VSCC grew they realised that there were some very good cars made in the 1930s, so they relented and decided on a classification for the better cars made between 1931 and 1939. These were called 'post-vintage thoroughbreds'.

In America the situation is chaotic because two different clubs classify cars from the same years in different ways. The oldest club, the Antique Automobile Club of America, formed in 1935, classifies cars made before 1930 as 'antiques', subdividing this with categories for 'veteran' cars running from 1906 to 1912 and 'vintage' cars from 1912 to 1929. The AACA classifies cars made from 1930 to 1942 as 'classic' cars, whereas, strangely, they call any vehicle more than 25 years old a 'production' vehicle.

Another American Club, the Horseless Car-

riage Club of America, calls cars made before 15 November 1915 'horseless carriages', whereas a newer club, the Classic Car Club of America, defines the classic years as running from 1925 to 1942. Nearly all American clubs are agreed that cars made before 1905 are 'pioneers'.

The dictionary definition of 'classic' is 'of the first class, of allowed excellence'. This is simple and to the point. Sadly, as far as the automobile world is concerned, the word has become somewhat debased over the years. Nowadays, advertisers will claim as a classic practically any car more than fifteen years old – even cars which were not very good when new and are now riddled with rust. In addition, they are at prices which would purchase a small house.

The word 'classic' is a suitable all-embracing term which can be used to describe a car of any age. Few owners would be foolish enough to call their fifteen-year-old car 'vintage' or 'antique', but 'classic' fits the bill nicely.

But what is a classic car? It is almost as difficult to define as it is to describe the specification of a sports car. Enthusiasts know instinctively that a Morgan, an Austin-Healey 3000 and a Jaguar E-type are all sports cars and that a Daimler SP250, a Chevrolet Camaro convertible and a Sunbeam Alpine are not. But how do you define that difference? I confess I do not know.

Equally, I could not define a classic car in words. Some might regard a classic as a vehicle built in small numbers and selling at a high price, giving rarity as their main definition. But there have been some very bad, expensive cars built in small numbers. However, I do not feel that a car has to be particularly good to rate as a classic, which is why I have included in this book cars like the Edsel, the Austin A90 Atlantic, de Tomaso Mangusta and Volkswagen Beetle.

This book is entitled *Classic Cars since 1945*, a contentious title to some people who believe that no classic cars have been built since World War II. This is nonsense, of course, as I have driven some wonderful cars built in the 1950s, 1960s and 1970s. Naturally, I have not been able to include every car that I would regard as a classic simply for reasons of space, and I hasten to point out that the selection of cars has been purely personal, so anyone who flies into a paroxysm of rage over the inclusion or omission of any particular car knows exactly who to blame. It is equally obvious, even to the tyro car enthusiast, that practically every Ferrari, Lamborghini, Jaguar, Aston Martin, Porsche, etc. has been a classic in no uncertain terms, but it would have been invidious and rather tedious to make the book top heavy with the *Grande Marques*, so lesser makes have been allowed to intrude where I think fit.

There have been enormous changes in the design of the motor car since the end of World War II – in fact it would probably be true to say that there have been more changes in the 35 years since the war than in the 50 or so years of car production before that war. Many enthusiasts would argue that a number of those changes have been for the worse. The onslaught of mass production methods has left us with look-alike cars all stamped from the same mould, in very thin rust-prone steel, leaving very little room for individual flair, except in exterior titivation and under-bonnet tuning. Even the latter pursuit is gradually being strangled by ever increasing legislation, limiting the noxious exhaust fumes, keeping our speeds down to safe limits and preventing us from being injured, should we run into each other.

But although we might pass dozens of other vehicles almost identical to our own, apart from colour, in the course of a short drive, who is to say

that modern cars are worse than their predecessors because of that? Certainly few drivers would like to go back to handling a Ford Popular or a Chevrolet Stylemaster on an everyday basis, but there is nothing at all wrong in keeping old objects even if they are not particularly valuable or of high quality. I know I remember the Ford Popular that I ran back in the 1950s with more affection than most cars I have driven since, simply because it was one of the first cars I owned and possibly because it was idiosyncratic. It was primitive by today's standards because it had no radio, heater, windscreen washers, or flashing direction indicators. The drum brakes made some slight impression on the leisurely forward progress, but not much; the gearbox had only three forward speeds, of which only the upper two had synchromesh; the side valve engine consumed fuel at a prodigious rate; the steering had about 3 inches of play at the wheel rim; the transverse leaf spring suspension allowed enormous angles of roll and the rigid axles front and rear transmitted every minor road blemish to the occupants. Yet I loved every minute at its wheel. For many people that's what makes a classic car, not high price or impeccable pedigree – simply nostalgia.

Mike Twite
Upper Benefield, 1981.

Horsepower Measurements
DIN: Deutsche Industrie Norm
SAE: Society of Automotive Engineers

Conversion Table

1 lb = 0.454 kg
1 pt = 0.568 l
1 gal (UK) = 4.544 l
1 cu in = 16.387 cc
1 in = 2.54 cm = 25.4 mm
$\frac{1}{4}$ mile = 400 m
1 mile = 1.609 km
1 mph = 1.609 kph
1 mpg (UK) = 0.354 km/l = 282.5 l/100 km
1 hp = 0.746 kW

FOREWORD

Most of us have happy memories of our earlier motoring days and as a motoring writer I have been fortunate to have had more opportunities to drive different cars than the majority of drivers. A few of the incidents among the many I can recall (some amusing some not) that have happened both to my colleagues and myself when driving some of the cars in this book may be of interest.

One motoring journalist of my acquaintance was testing an Allard J2, attempting to see how fast it would go on the Southend Arterial road. About half a mile ahead a Morris 8 travelling at 30 mph pulled out to overtake an Austin 7 doing 29½ mph and, despite frantic application of the brakes, the Allard ploughed into the rear of the Morris. The Morris shot off up the road and came to rest on the central reservation about a quarter of a mile away. The journalist rushed up to the car expecting to find a dead body, but the driver was laying on his back in the rear of the car (the driving seat having broken clean off its mountings) with a blissful smile on his face. Asked why he was smiling after having had his car destroyed he said, 'It's the first time I've ever done 70 in this car!'

The practice of using the drive shaft as a member of the suspension has never seemed good engineering practice to me and this was confirmed when a colleague and I were testing a Chevrolet Corvette Stingray. After testing the car at speeds up to 140 mph I got out of the car to visit a printer while my colleague continued his journey. Soon afterwards I had a telephone call from him asking me to rescue him as he had had an 'incident'. When I arrived I found the car leaning drunkenly against the kerb, with lots of exciting looking black marks leading up to the rear of the car. What had happened was that the drive shaft had snapped at its outer end, allowing the wheel to collapse inwards; the flailing end of the shaft carried on rotating, clearing away much of the rear bodywork, the fuel tank and brake piping. Luckily the road was straight, there was no traffic about and my colleague had only been doing about 60 mph. Shortly before, we had been doing 140 mph! To be fair, I have never heard of a similar incident on either the Corvette or the E-type Jaguar which use similar suspension layouts.

I once took a Daimler SP250 to a photographic assignment soon after its introduction, and was a little put out to have the driver's door fly open as I rounded a left-hand bend. The photographer laughed, but the smile was soon wiped off his face when I nipped round a right-hand bend quite smartly and his door flew open! This was of course in the days before safety belts became compulsory!

I ran two Sprites and enjoyed them more than any other cars I have owned. The first was stolen and when it was found over a year later it was *better* than when I had lost it. The new 'owner' had fitted wider wheels, had tuned the engine and modified the suspension. Sadly, by then it belonged to the insurance company as they had paid out long before.

I had the pleasure of driving a Ford GT 40 for two weeks as an everyday car and I must admit I could hardly be prised out of it to do any work! My first drive in the Mk-I was undertaken in damp weather and at first I was impressed with the way it behaved on soaking wet roads, but after an hour or so I became aware of a numbness in my nether regions. I put this down to the less than luxurious seating but as the numbness crept higher I became alarmed. Glancing down, I suddenly realised that I was sitting in about three inches of water! From then on, I placed a thick plastic bag on the seat and tucked my trousers into my socks. I suppose if I had paid £5000 for it I would have been annoyed but it seemed amusing at the time.

During my early morning speed checks on the M1 (before the 70 mph speed limit, by the way) I was pulled up by a police car, the driver of which said that a member of the public had stopped at a motorway telephone to report that he had been overtaken by a 'white sports car doing 200 mph'. Since the car was a sort of greeny-gold metallic colour the policeman admitted that he could have got the wrong car and put his notebook away. He walked away a few steps then returned, smiling, and said, 'Now sir, as a private citizen I would like to know what she'll do!'

The GT40 has a fairly heavy appetite for fuel – I averaged about 15 mpg during my stint. On one occasion I pulled up at a small garage in Scotland to fill up and asked the owner to fill her up. He managed to squeeze 15 gallons into the tank and his dour face was beginning to crack into a smile at the thought of the profit he was going to make. When I pointed to the *other* filler cap on the opposite side of the car and asked him to fill that too he practically danced over! He ended up putting 33 gallons into the tanks!

I once took my Jaguar E-type down to Italy on holiday and parked outside my hotel between a Mercedes-Benz 230SL, which had only been introduced a few months before, and a Fiat 124 twin-cam. On the beach a few days later I was approached by the owners of both the Mercedes and the Fiat and after a little skirmishing to discover which language we should converse in, ending up with German, the Mercedes owner pointed across the road to my E-type and asked how much power. Knowing that his Mercedes gave *only* 150 bhp, I told him 265 bhp. His expression hardened. Then he asked me what the top speed was. When I said 250 kph, he muttered to himself and after a little more desultry conversation he made off, while the Italian sat there grinning. He just enjoyed fast cars no matter where they were made. I quite enjoyed being British that day!

I have had many glorious drives in Porsche 911s, none more interesting than in a Targa I took down to Italy in order to visit the Lamborghini factory where I was to test a new Lamborghini. The Lamborghini people asked me to leave the keys of the Porsche with them while I tested the Lamborghini; I thought nothing of this at the time but when I returned and found the Porsche parked in a different place and with quite a few more miles on the clock, I started asking questions and found that not only had they driven the car but they had taken one or two bits to pieces to find how they worked! I did not know it then but they were just starting work on their own 'small' car, the Urraco. Mind you, when I took the then brand new Jaguar XJ6 to the Porsche factory and left it there for a few days they confessed that they had done a little more than just lift the bonnet!

I have been privileged to drive several Lamborghini models, many of them at the Bologna factory. The invariable routine when trying cars in Italy was to get up at around 5 am and take the car out on to a near-deserted stretch of Autostrada. First, we would calibrate the speedometer against the kilometre posts, then we would try to discover the maximum speed of the car; this involved driving for many miles on flat stretches of the motorway, watching the speed gradually creep up until it stabilised. When we had established the top speed in this direction we would turn round and repeat the operation in the opposite direction. There is no particular skill involved in driving at 170 mph on a deserted motorway, but the driver does have to watch out for gusts of wind, which become very important at those speeds, while a Fiat 500 spotted half a mile ahead in the slow lane is already a potential hazard.

Sadly, I once did something extremely foolish in an ISO Grifo at a test session at Silverstone racing circuit. I was enjoying myself rushing round the track in the car, finding the road-holding on a race track just as delightful as on the road. I arrived at the fairly tight Becketts corner on one lap and the gear lever jumped out of third gear, but no harm was done and I put it back into gear. I should have slowed right down then and there but I was enjoying myself too much and I rushed down to the fast Stowe corner, changed down into third again at around 100 mph and turned into the bend. Just as I was about to put the power on again the car suddenly turned sideways and charged the heavy brick wall on the inside of the circuit. It flew through the wall, with bricks hurtling through the air and came to rest with the car well and truly wrecked. When I recovered my senses I looked down at the gear lever and saw that it was in neutral! It had jumped out of gear again and I learned a very expensive lesson. Later on I was talking to a colleague about the accident and I told him what had happened. 'Oh, it jumped out of gear when I was driving it,' he said, 'but I just thought I hadn't engaged it properly.'

POSTWAR AUSTERITY

Like several immediately post-war cars, the Armstrong-Siddeley Hurricane was named after a famous aeroplane. This is a 1949 example.

POSTWAR AUSTERITY

At the end of World War II the world's motor industry was in tatters – in fact only in the USA had car production been carried on at all on any large scale, while in other countries most car factories had been all but destroyed. In Britain, the centre of the motor industry in Coventry and Birmingham had suffered a tremendous pounding, and in Germany, the Mercedes factory hardly had a wall still standing.

Not only were factories damaged, but there were no cars to make anyway. The majority of factories had been engaged in war production and the type of production line necessary to build tanks or aircraft parts was hardly conducive to the building of cars.

Despite these tremendous handicaps the big car companies slowly struggled back to life. They had to, because no one wanted the tanks, guns and bombs they had been making during the war and the demand for new cars was insatiable. Many thousands of cars had been destroyed during the war and those that remained commanded enormous prices, often double their new price before the war.

In the USA conditions were not quite as rosy as might have appeared from its distance from war-torn Europe. Although US industry was not ravaged by strategic bombing, her economy had suffered from the ceaseless production of war material, much of which was never paid for by her European allies. There were many shortages, and steel, glass, copper and rubber were often in short supply. The trade unions began to flex their muscles and long strikes were common in the motor industry.

Even so, the US industry was turning out cars by the million in 1945 and exporting them around the world in ever increasing numbers. The basic American car of the late 1940s could hardly be termed a classic, consisting of a separate chassis into which was fitted a straight six, side valve engine of around 4-litre (240 cu in) capacity, mated to a three-speed column shift gearbox. The bodywork was pre-war in style, but the cars gave Americans what they needed at that time: effortless high speed cruising and plenty of space.

The MG TC was based on the pre-war TA and TB, but became the classic of that Midget series.

The classic American cars of pre-war years were already but a memory and only a few far-sighted collectors were saving such classics as Auburn, Cord, Duesenberg, Marmom, Mercer, Pierce-Arrow, and Stutz from the breakers' yards. The emphasis was once again on cars for the masses, and production roared on to such an extent that the US industry produced 6.6 million cars in 1950.

In Britain most car manufacturers saw that the tide of war was turning in the Allies favour during late 1944, and many began making plans for post-war production. The Austin Motor Co. Ltd was the first to make its plans public, announcing a range of four cars in November 1944. There was no question of producing these cars until the war was won, and in August 1945 the plant went over to car production with the Austin Eight, Ten, Twelve, and Sixteen. The first three were cars which had been in production in 1939, but the Sixteen was a new car, using a 2.2-litre engine developed from a military engine.

Virtually all other British manufacturers recommended production with pre-war designs and it was left to the relatively small firm of Armstrong Siddeley of Coventry to announce the first really new British car after the war. In May 1945 they showed the Lancaster and Hurricane to the public, both cars being named after wartime aircraft. The Lancaster was a four-door saloon, whereas the Hurricane was a two-door drophead coupé of stunning good looks, which has endowed it with classic status among British enthusiasts. Mechanically it was not outstanding even for 1945. It features a separate chassis frame with underslung leaf springs at the rear and independent front suspension by upper wishbones and a single lower link operating torsion bars. Power comes from a straight-six engine of

The war may have delayed development of the VW 'Beetle', but it did nothing to hamper sales and this amazing car is still in production in some countries. This is a 1950 version.

2-litre (120 cu in) capacity, developing a maximum power of 70 bhp. Buyers could opt for a four-speed all synchromesh gearbox or the Wilson pre-selector gearbox which had been a hallmark of Armstrong Siddeleys for many years.

The Armstrong Siddeley was a quality car vying with Rover and Alvis for its clientele, so naturally only the best wood and leather trimming was used, while such extras as a radio and interior heater were catalogued (almost unheard of in British cars of the era, although they were commonplace in the USA).

The sculptured styling of the Hurricane differed from most other British cars of the time in having headlamps recessed into the front wings and a radiator grille that was very modern in design, although a stylised version of the traditional Sphinx mascot sat atop the alligator bonnet.

The Hurricane and its sister models became available with a 2309cc version of the straight-six engine in 1949, which raised peak power to 75 brake horse power. With a weight of around $1\frac{1}{2}$ tons the Hurricane was no high performer and was happiest cruising in the middle 60s, although it had a top speed of just over 70 mph. The Hurricane, Lancaster and the later two-door saloon model, the Typhoon (named after the Hawker fighter aircraft), continued in production until 1953, at which point over 12,000 had been built.

The engine of the Armstrong Siddeley highlights one of the problems that the British industry had to labour under in the post-war period. The Government in its wisdom had instituted a form of taxation based on the bore of the engine cylinders, and the greater the bore the more annual car tax owners paid. In an effort to circumvent this problem engine designers built engines with as narrow a bore as possible and long strokes. Thus the Hurricane had a bore of 65 mm and a stroke of 100 mm, which meant that it was a low revving unit, from which it was difficult to extract good power outputs. Other countries had no such deterrents and could build much more modern engines.

The tax was known as the RAC Tax because the Royal Automobile Club calculated the tax rating of each new model, so cars became known by their RAC rating rather than their model name, although many makers named their cars after their RAC ratings, such as the Morris 8 and 10 or Austin Eight, Ten, Twelve and Sixteen. The RAC tax was discontinued in 1947.

The very fact that motorists had sufficient money to buy a new car in post-war Britain could not guarantee them a car, because one had to obtain a licence to show that it was necessary for business reasons. Even with the licence in your hand a wait of several months was inevitable; and the introduction of Purchase Tax made the financial outlay crippling. The Government constantly berated the motor industry to produce more cars and to export more. In 1946 an export target of 100,000 cars was set for the British motor industry, but it only managed to build 147,767 in total! The catchphrase 'export or die' was coined to persuade every industry that Britain could only survive by exporting large percentages of its total production.

This constant barrage of propaganda persuaded many car manufactureres to export cars which had not been sufficiently tested for the markets for which they were destined. Cars with inefficient heaters were sent to cold countries, cars with poor body sealing were exported to dusty countries and in nearly every case poor sales and service networks left customers without their cars for long periods.

Even in the USA the car makers were not without problems, for the Government insisted that they make only 200 000 cars in 1945 and that the price of cars should be 2 per cent less than the equivalent car cost in 1942. So some makers sold their cars at a loss.

Despite the restrictions and the lack of raw materials manufacturers gradually got into their stride, not only with basic transport but also with sports cars and high quality machines. One of the first of these was announced in November 1945, a car whose influence reached far beyond the mere 10,003 it sold before being replaced. This was the MG TC, from the tiny factory at Abingdon. Based on the pre-war TA and TB, the TC was improved in small but important respects, such as a four-inch increase in body width and the use of a new synchromesh gearbox. But essentially it was unchanged, with a typical pre-war ladder type chassis, open two-seater bodywork, a $13\frac{1}{2}$-gallon slab fuel tank hung on the back, 18-in wire

The Citröen Light 15 pioneered the use of front-wheel drive in mass production and set a standard for many years.

wheels, with power coming from the little 1250cc engine. This engine had been developed from the M-series Morris Ten engine, and with bore and stroke of 66.5 mm by 90 mm the engine developed 54.5 bhp using twin SU carburettors and a compression ratio of 7.2:1. With a dry weight of only 15½ cwt the TC was quite a quick car for 1945, accelerating to 50 mph from a standstill in under 15 seconds and going on to a top speed of 80 mph.

It was in its cornering, steering and braking, however, that the TC impressed most. The firm suspension gave a rough ride on poor roads up to about 40 mph but with its high geared steering it could be flicked through bends incredibly quickly.

Many millions of American servicemen had passed through Britain on their way to and from the war between 1942 and 1945 and many of them had taken note of the small European spors cars that seemed to stick to the road like a postage stamp. When MG TCs began arriving in the States they were snapped up by enthusiasts who were delighted with the quick responses of the little car. Compared with the average American sedan, with its sloppy ride, low geared steering and soggy behaviour on corners the TC was a revelation. Almost alone, the TC was responsible for converting American drivers to the more responsive type of European car, persuading several notable drivers to take up motor racing, including 1961 World Champion Phil Hill, and even the formation of several sports car magazines. Yet only 2000 cars were exported to the USA! Nevertheless those 2000 formed the nucleus of the Sports Car Club of America and converted the country to road racing.

There were plenty of tuning parts available for the TC and the MG factory supplied kits of parts and even provided a tuning manual. Some of the cars tuned in the late 1940s are still racing today.

On a more prosaic note, a little economy car was struggling to be reborn in the town of Wolfsburg in shattered Germany. This was, of course, the Volkswagen, or People's Car, which Adolf Hitler had first proposed in the 1930s. His idea was to put a car outside every house in Germany and by specifying a simple design that could be built in vast quantities he hoped to sell them at an incredibly low price. The great engineer Dr Ferdinand Porsche was put to work designing the car and he came up with a surprisingly advanced design, which was to have far-reaching effects on the world's motor industry. The war interrupted Hitler's plan to swamp Germany with Beetles, as the little black cars became known, and war production was centred on military versions such as the *Kübelwagen* and amphibious *Schwimmwagen*.

In 1945 Wolfsburg fell into the British sector of West Germany and the British Army were given the task of evaluating the Beetle to discover if it was a viable vehicle. To their discredit they dismissed it as a rough, noisy, cramped vehicle with no particular merit, and left it to the Germans. Dr Heinz Nordhoff took over the Volkswagen factory and with a dedicated workforce began assembling Beetles at an ever-increasing rate. Today, the car is still in production around the world, having long ago become the world's best selling car, surpassing the 14 million plus achieved by the Model T Ford in the 1920s.

The basis of the Volkswagen was a flat platform chassis mated to a central backbone to which the body was bolted after the mechanical components had been fitted. Instead of the front engine, rigid axles and old fashioned leaf springs that were common in the 1930s, Dr Porsche designed an all-independent suspension, with swing axles at the rear located by trailing arms, whereas at the front twin trailing arms were used with springing front and rear by transverse torsion bars. Drum brakes were fitted on all four wheels and steering was by worm and roller.

Perhaps the most ingenious part of the car was the simple air-cooled horizontally-opposed four-cylinder engine which in original form had a bore and stroke of 75 mm × 64 mm for a capacity of 1131cc, but the bore was increased to 77 mm for a capacity of 1192cc. This engine developed a modest 25 bhp at 3300 rpm in original form, but although this endowed the car with modest acceleration, once it achieved its cruising speed it was able to hold it all day with no sign of stress. The engine was mated to a four-speed transaxle unit, originally with no synchromesh, and 6-volt electrics were fitted.

Although the car was advanced in many ways it

could be built cheaply because of many cost-cutting design features. The brakes were cable-operated at a time when hydraulic brakes were quite common; there was no water-cooling system to worry about; heating was achieved by ducting air from around the exhaust manifolds; instrumentation was kept to the absolute minimum. On early cars there was not even a petrol gauge, simply a reserve tank. When the engine began to splutter you operated the reserve tank lever and headed for a garage!

The British Army experts had been right about the Beetle, it *was* rough, noisy and cramped, but it went on going long after other cars had been consigned to the scrapheap. The thickness of the body steel and the excellent paintwork gave it a very long life and the excellent fit of the panels meant that owners very often had to open a window before the doors would shut, and there are many stories of VWs being caught in floods and floating happily for hours until dry land was reached. One owner even fitted a propellor to the rear of the gearbox and drove across the English Channel! The British concessionaries were so impressed by the reliability of the car that they gave certificates and badges to owners who had covered 100,000 miles in their cars, but by the early 1960s they were giving away so many badges every week that they abandoned the scheme.

Of course, the Beetle had drawbacks. There was not much room under the front mounted bonnet, the cornering power was a bit suspect, as the rear swing axles tended to jack up under heavy cornering, and the body shape did not respond well to crosswinds on motorways. The engine was also rather inaccessible, but a trained mechanic could remove the engine in twenty minutes.

It may seem odd to credit the Beetle with classic status, but it was a brilliant design that changed the whole world of motoring for it spawned many imitators, some of which still linger on today. In Italy, Fiat designed a whole range of rear-engined cars such as the 500, 600 and 850. In France Renault built the 4CV followed by the Dauphine, Floride, Caravelle and R8, while Simca built the 1000, which is still made today. In the USA, General Motors scaled up the Beetle design for the Chevrolet Corvair, a

car which cost GM a great deal of money when
Ralph Nader launched his safety campaign, with
the unsafe handling characteristics of the Corvair
as his main weapon. In a way, Nader may
ultimately be responsible for elevating the
Corvair to classic status.

In France, Citröen were quietly restarting
production in late 1945 with a car of a type that
had been in production since 1934. Known in
France as the 11CV , but in Britain as the Light
15, this car was exceptional in that it drove its
front wheels. Few 1945 motorist could visualise
that front-wheel drive would sweep the world
within three decades, virtually ousting the rear-
engined car from the roads. At that time the
Citröen was regarded as a slightly eccentric car
for the better off enthusiast and not as potential
transport for the masses.

None of the features of the Light 15 were
revolutionary, and all had been used on other cars
in the past, but the combination of design
features put it far ahead of its contemporaries.

The chassis/body unit was of unitary construction with a flat floor, to which was welded
the scuttle structure and main body panels. At the
front, two welded steel structures projected
forwards to hold the front suspension and engine
unit. Suspension at the front was independent by
torsion bars, whereas at the rear a dead beam axle
mounted on torsion bars was used. The four-
cylinder water-cooled engine was mounted
behind the gearbox and, as the engine had to be in
full view under the bonnet for servicing, this
made for a lengthy car, which was one of the
drawbacks of the original design. With a wheel-
base of 9 ft $6\frac{1}{2}$ in and an over-all length of 14 ft 5 in
the Light 15 was fairly large even by the
standards of the day. The transmission layout of
the Light 15 was quite complicated as the
differential was fitted between the engine and
gearbox. Power was taken from the engine
through the clutch to the gearbox via a primary
shaft, then back to the differential through the
secondary shaft. Drive was taken to the front
wheels via universally-jointed cardan shafts,
with constant velocity outer joints. Despite its

*Styling of the Triumph Roadster was unashamedly
American. This 2-litre example of 1948 is pictured
with the 'dickey' seat in the working position.*

complexity the Light 15 was generally reliable and owners would not normally be aware that the car was driven by its front wheels. More enterprising owners found that the car would run wide on bends if the throttle foot was lifted and most owners complained about the heavy steering and poor gearchange; the latter was operated by a dashboard mounted lever which tended to be rather vague when called upon to select one of the three gears.

The 1911cc engine gave 56 bhp in 1945, which would propel the Light 15 to about 75 mph, although acceleration was quite leisurely because of the weight of the car. For some time after the war the Light 15 was only available in black, just like the Model T Ford. It remained largely unchanged throughout its life, going out of production in 1955. It was supplemented by the Big 15, which was much the same apart from the 7-in increase in wheelbase, while the Six model used the Big 15 chassis in conjunction with a 76 bhp six-cylinder version of the Light 15 engine.

The Light 15's influence came not from vast sales (only just over 700,000 were built) but from its success as a production car, proving that front-wheel drive, torsion bar suspension and unitary construction were viable propositions. Its 'wheel at each corner' suspension system endowed the car with the sort of cornering ability which is commendable even today, and the torsion bar springing coped with the atrocious roads of post-war France in an enviable way.

In Britain, 1946 brought the announcement of a new sports roadster which helped to dispel the gloom of the war years and to show that austerity motoring was not going to be the lot of every motorist. This car was the Triumph Roadster, which was developed from the 1800 saloon.

That Triumph were making any cars at all was remarkable because the company had got into severe financial difficulties before the war and had to call in the receiver. After brief attempts to merge with Riley, Triumph was taken over by a steel firm, Thomas Ward, who planned to resume

The classic Bristol 400, the first car from that company, bore a very close resemblance to the pre-war BMW range. In four years only 700 examples were made.

This is the coupé version of the Arnolt-Bristol, an Anglo-American concoction with Italian coachwork.

car manufacture. The war intervened, however, and the factory was turned over to building Mosquito aircraft. Like the rest of Coventry it was badly damaged during the war, but in 1944 Sir John Black of the Standard Motor Company bought Triumph and they were back in production by early 1946.

The chassis of the 1800 saloon and roadster were virtually identical, except for the obvious differences of steering column rake, seating positions etc. The chassis consisted of a pair of $3\frac{1}{2}$-in diameter steel tubes, liberally strengthened by cross members and sheet steel pressings. The rear of the chassis was underslung beneath the rear axle to give a low build and the axle was supported on leaf springs. At the front, suspension was independent with wishbones and a transverse leaf spring. Braking was all drum by the new Girling Hydrostatic system in which the

linings were in light contact with the drum and were self adjusting.

The overhead valve engine was developed from that of the Standard 14/12, the four-cylinder engine having a capacity of 1776cc and developing a modest 65 bhp at 4500 rpm using a single Solex carburettor and a compression ratio of 6.72:1 to cope with the dreadful 'Pool' petrol then available in Britain. It was another long stroke engine to cater for the iniquitous RAC horsepower tax and was therefore not a high revving unit. However, in the Roadster it was capable of 75 mph even though the car weighed well in excess of a ton.

The bodywork was unashamedly aimed at the American market, the bulbous front wings and curved rear end being not unattractive for all that. The bench seat to take three passengers was all-American, as was the right-hand steering column gear change lever. Even more American was the 'rumble' or 'dickey' seat in the tail which was reached by lifting a lid, then climbing up on a step. The lid had glass panels inserted and was left in the raised position when the rumble seat was occupied to give the occupants some protection. With the hood raised the rumble seat occupants stayed out in the rain!

As its name suggests the Roadster was not really a sports car and it did not attract true enthusiasts away from MGs, Morgans and the like. They detested the bench seat and the column change, which developed considerable play in its labyrinth of rods and levers. Nevertheless, it attracted a small but enthusiastic clientele of its own and is now much sought after by collectors.

The Roadster continued in 1800cc form until October 1948 when it was replaced by the 2000 Roadster. The owners of the Triumph factory, the Standard Motor Company, had introduced the Standard Vanguard and in an effort to standardise their range the 2088cc 68 bhp Vanguard engine, three-speed gearbox and rear axle were fitted to an otherwise unchanged Roadster. This combination had a better top gear performance than the 1800, but a three-speed gearbox did not appeal to many and the model was dropped after only a year in production. A total of only 4500 Roadsters were built in all, but a modern buyer can expect to pay at least twice as much as its first owner paid. The saloon version of the Roadster, the Renown, is also becoming something of a collector's item, largely because of its 'razor edge' styling.

It was difficult enough for old established car manufacturers to pick up the threads at the end of the war but for a brand new firm it would have seemed almost impossible. In 1945, however, the Bristol Aeroplane Company formed a Car Division. They decided to aim for the luxury Grand Touring market and rather than design and build a complete car from scratch they decided to use the pre-war BMW range as the basis for their new model. One of the Bristol

directors had been a director of AFN Ltd who imported BMW cars before the war so cars and engines as well as drawings and know-how were made available. With their considerable aircraft engine experience Bristol made a number of improvements on the 328 BMW engine, but still retained the excellent hemispherical combustion chamber layout with its unusual cross pushrods to operate the exhaust valves. This six-cylinder 1971cc engine developed 80 bhp with a single Solex carburettor, but this was replaced by three SU carburettors before long, which raised power to 85 bhp. The four-speed gearbox was unusual in having a freewheel arrangement on first gear.

The chassis of the 400 was fabricated from steel box sections and the independent front suspension was by upper wishbones, with a transverse leaf spring acting as the lower link, while the rigid rear axle was suspended on torsion bars.

Bodywork of the 400 was more than reminiscent of the BMW, the radiator grille being very similar to the 'double oval' shape used by BMW. The body shape was a halfway house between the pre-war style of separate wings and running boards and the more modern shapes that followed. The front wings were flared into the bodywork and the 'running boards' sloped far too much to be used as such.

Production of the 400, which had started in 1947, continued until early 1951, but the pace of development at Bristol did not stand still and new models appeared almost every year thereafter. The power output of the engine was increased considerably, so much so that several racing car manufacturers such as Frazer-Nash, Cooper, Lister and Lotus used the engine with great success. Bristol developed their own racing coupé and were very successful in long distance races such as the Le Mans 24 Hour race.

No Bristol was ever cheap and the price of the 400 at £2400 deterred all but the wealthiest owner. Not surprisingly only 700 examples of the 400 were produced.

An interesting Bristol model was the Arnolt-Bristol which was designed for export only. An American car importer, S. H. 'Wacky' Arnolt, approached Bristol to provide chassis to which he could have special bodies fitted. They agreed to this and provided the 404 with a tuned 125 bhp

version of the 2-litre engine. The chassis were
sent to the Italian bodybuilder Bertone who fitted
them with a simple two-seater open body before
shipping them to New York for completion. A
coupé version of the same model was introduced
in 1955. Because Italian bodywork was cheaper
than British bodywork at that time, the Arnolt-
Bristol sold for $4250 in the USA in 1953,
considerably less than the standard 404 cost in
Britain. Although production was never high the
Arnolt-Bristol continued until 1961 when the
faithful 2-litre engine was dropped in favour of
the Canadian built Chrysler 5.2-litre V8.

In 1948 a new British car appeared on world
markets creating as much if not more furore in
the USA as the MG TC had three years before.
This was of course the Jaguar XK120.

The story of how Sir William Lyons, Bill
Heynes and Claude Baily sat together on the roof
of Jaguar's Coventry factory and designed the
XK120 whilst fire watching during German
bombing raids has been told many times.
Naturally, they did not actually design it up
there, but they laid down the basic format of their
post-war range, which was put into fruition as
soon as hostilities ended.

The heart of the XK120 was its engine, which
was a completely new design. It was designed by
Heynes, Baily and Walter Hassan, with combustion expert Harry Weslake being retained to
oversee cylinder head design. It was thoroughly
modern in design with twin overhead camshafts
in a light alloy cylinder head, driven by chains.
The valves were set at a 70° angle for perfect
hemispherical shape and carburation was by twin
SUs. The crankshaft was a massive forging with
seven main bearings and the 3442cc six-cylinder
unit gave 160 bhp at 5000 rpm on a modest 7:1
compression ratio.

The chassis into which the engine was placed
was not particularly advanced, having a box
section frame with deep box section crossmem-
bers to add strength. Suspension was similar to
that of the Mk V saloon with torsion bar
independent front suspension and a rigid rear
axle mounted on leaf springs. Steering was by

*The standard British Bristol 404, on which the
Arnolt-Bristol was based; this is a 1954 version.*

The start of a legend: Jaguar's superb XK120 was announced in 1948 and set the style for a long series which followed. The XK engine is still in use into the 1980s.

recirculating ball and the Lockheed drum brakes had a massive 12-in diameter. The engine drove through the Moss four-speed gearbox with synchromesh on the top three ratios.

It was the bodywork which formed the main attraction of the XK120, for by the standards of 1948 it was sleek and *avant garde*. The fully enclosed front wings framed inset headlamps and an oval radiator grille, while the wings swept backwards to the spatted rear wheels. The split-vee windscreen completed the *ensemble*.

When announced in 1948 the XK120 created a sensation, so in advance of its time was it in many ways. Independent road tests soon demonstrated that the 120 of its title was no misnomer, for several journals recorded top speeds of around 124 mph, while Jaguar themselves took a car to Belgium, fitted it with an undertray, removed the hood and windscreen and drove it through a flying mile at 132.596 mph. With hood and screen replaced it still covered the same distance at 126.448 mph.

The car was not without faults, however, and testers commented on the tendency of the brakes to fade, of road shocks to be transmitted to the steering, and a softness in the suspension that was treated with suspicion by testers brought up in the belief that sports cars *had* to have stiff suspension.

The overwhelming factor in favour of the XK120 was its price. In Britain it retailed for £1273, while in the States it could be had for $4000. So great was the demand in the USA that virtually the whole production went there in the first year or so, and indeed less than 10 per cent of the entire production of XK120s right up to the end in 1954 stayed in Britain, which possibly helps to explain the enormous prices asked for them today!

In 1951 the open version was joined by a fixed head coupé model, which many felt to be even more attractive than the convertible, while in 1953 a drophead coupé was announced. This had a much superior folding hood and proper wind-up windows, unlike the convertible which had

The Porsche 356 was closely based on the VW Beetle. It was made in numerous versions between 1950 and 1965. The car shown is the fifth eldest survivor.

*Announced in 1948, the Alec Issigonis designed
Morris Minor found immediate and enduring
popularity. The car was available during its
production run of over a million cars in saloon,
tourer, and the popular 'countryman' estate.*

The hardtop version of Austin's A90 Atlantic was longer lived than its convertible brother, continuing for two years after the soft-top's demise at the end of 1950. The car was designed especially with the US market in mind.

sidescreens.

Despite its fairly 'soft' image the XK120 did well in racing and rallying, prompting Jaguar to introduce the XK120C (or C type as it is better known) which was a 210 bhp racing two-seater using XK120 components. Despite the fact that it had the power to win the Le Mans race it was a catalogued model and could be bought for around £2200.

Another variant of the 120 was the XK120M which was available for the American market only and featured an engine tuned to give 180 bhp plus various other performance extras.

The XK120 gave way to the XK140 in October 1954 and with 190 bhp, rack and pinion steering, firmer suspension and improved brakes this was in many ways better than the XK120, with no increase in weight to hamper it. However, the shape was no longer unusual by 1954 and it did not have the same impact, while the later XK150, was heavier, uglier and slower.

The XK120 started a glorious tradition for Jaguar and for more than ten years Jaguar owners and racing drivers were the envy of their fellows. The only fly in the ointment for road going XK owners was that Jaguar's effective cost cutting exercises tended to trim quality as well so that the cars often suffered niggling faults. As one American owner said, 'I loved that Jaguar. Nothing went wrong with the engine or gearbox but the darned thing nickel and dimed me to death.'

Another British model which looked as if it could sweep the world was announced in 1948. This was the Morris Minor, successor to the pre-war Morris Minors. Designed by Alec Issigonis, it was a much more modern car than its predecessors and indeed many of its contemporaries. It would have been even further ahead had its designer been given permission to develop his design with a free hand but financial considerations prevented him from doing this. He had to wait a further eleven years to see his ideas come to fruition.

Morris Motors badly needed a modern car to replace their basically pre-war Eight Series E and Ten Series M cars, as by 1948 they were looking dated. Issigonis set out to design a small car which could carry four or five people comfortably, yet have the handling of a sports car. He

wanted to use an air-cooled flat four power unit to get a low bonnet line and he wanted to use front-wheel drive so that the cabin could have a flat unobstructed floor. Unfortunately, Morris Motors could not finance a complete new car and it is doubtful whether British industry had the technology at the time to design a front-wheel-drive layout suitable for mass production.

So Issigonis had to be content with the old side valve engine and gearbox from the Morris Eight and in the absence of front-wheel drive was obliged to use a live rear axle mounted on leaf springs. However, at the front he used a clever independent suspension layout which utilized lower wishbones attached to longitudinal torsion bars with the upper location being looked after by the arm of a lever arm shock absorber.

The bulbous two door body/chassis unit was a unit construction type welded up from steel pressings. Morris had installed the American Budd integral body/chassis system before the war and although they had suffered a lot of teething troubles it worked well in the Minor, which was light yet very rigid.

The car was an immediate success with the public, even those to whom good handling was not a prerequisite, because the car felt safe under all conditions. The rack and pinion steering (unusual on a small car in 1948) was light and required only 2½ turns lock to lock. The side valve engine produced only 27.5 bhp from its 918cc and top speed barely surpassed 60 mph, but so good was the handling that the car could maintain its top speed around surprisingly tight bends.

In February 1952 Austin and the Nuffield Group (Morris, Riley, Wolseley, and MG) merged to form the British Motor Corporation and one of the first acts was to fit the Minor with the engine from the Austin A30. Although this engine was only of 830cc it was more modern, had overhead valves and gave 30 bhp. Top speed rose slightly, to 63 mph and fuel consumption remained at a commendable 40 mpg.

The original two-door saloon had been joined by a convertible soon afterwards and by a four-door saloon version in 1950.

There was a vogue for wood-framed station wagons in the 1950s and BMC cashed in on this by announcing the Minor Traveller in 1953. This

featured an estate car tail section with two vertically split rear doors and ash framing on the outside of the bodywork, rather like a Tudor house.

In October 1956 the Series II Minor was replaced by the Minor 1000 range, which was identical to its predecessor except that the split windscreen had been replaced by a single piece screen together with a matching rear window. Mechanically, the engine was replaced by the 948cc 'A' series engine which gave 37 bhp and a top speed in excess of 70 mph. A higher rear axle ratio enabled it to retain its 40 mpg fuel consumption.

In January 1961 the Minor became the first British model to exceed the 1,000,000 production mark and to commemorate the event BMC produced a special version called the Morris Million which was painted a pale lilac colour. Unfortunately, they made 371 of them so the

This Austin A40 Sports is shown competing on the London Rally of 1952. This Jensen-bodied car did not capture the imagination of the American public at which it was aimed.

model is not quite as exclusive as it might be.

The Minor continued in production until 1970 by which time it was using the 1098cc 'A' series engine which gave 48 bhp at 5100 rpm. There was quite an uproar from the British public when the model was dropped and there was a small rush to obtain one of the final few, while one garage man even went so far as to build up a complete car from stocks of spares held in his stores.

Since its demise the Minor has become something of a cult car and the split-screen versions made until 1956 are becoming collector's items, especially the Convertible and

AC built sporting saloons, as well as outright sportsters. This is the Greyhound of 1956, which was powered by a 2.2-litre Bristol engine.

Traveller models, despite their tendency to rot rather badly. A cottage industry has sprung up in England, with small firms doing nothing but restoration work on Morris Minors, some of the firms doing total rebuilds at horrific cost. As the Minor is now regarded as a classic, however, many investors no doubt feel that the outlay is worthwhile.

In the same year that the Morris Minor was announced, 1948, in the town of Gmund in Austria a hardly less momentous occasion was being enacted. Dr Ferry Porsche, son of Dr Ferdinand Porsche who designed the Volkswagen, was building a sports car. Both of the Porsches had been imprisoned at the end of the war, but Ferry was released before his father and went to Gmund, as the company was not allowed to restart work at their old factory in Zuffenhausen, a suburb of Stuttgart.

There were many wartime Volkswagen vehicles about at the end of the war and few people knew how to repair them, so it was natural for many of them to be taken to Ferry Porsche in Gmund where he gradually built up a repair business.

With various parts from old Volkswagens, Porsche designed a chassis, with the 1131 cc VW engine mounted at the rear. The suspension, braking and steering were all VW parts but the engine was tuned to give about 40 bhp. A very simple open two-seater body was fitted and after some local testing the prototype was sold to a Swiss enthusiast. This car was tested by a Swiss motoring magazine and soon orders began to roll in. Export licences were difficult to come by and only 50 handbuilt cars were made with aluminium bodywork before a contract was arranged with an outside bodywork builder to build a drophead coupé version.

Production was eventually moved back to Stuttgart and by 1950 the new car, known as the 356, was in full production, with the bodies being made at the nearby Reutter works. The engine had been reduced in capacity to 1086cc, but it still

Armstrong-Siddeley built many luxurious saloons, such as this 4-litre Star Sapphire of 1956; like several other models, this was available only with automatic transmission.

gave 40 bhp at 4200 rpm and had a top speed of 85 mph. Despite the shortcomings of the VW suspension and poor braking, enthusiasts recognised the superb qualities of this little car that could run rings round bigger sports cars.

Finance was building up well, as the burgeoning VW factory at Wolfsburg was paying Dr Porsche royalties on every VW made, so many improvements were made to the 356. It soon had better brakes (courtesy of Lockheed in England), bigger engines and much improved handling and steering. In 1951 buyers had the choice of the original 1086cc engine plus a 44 bhp 1286cc unit and a 60 bhp 1488cc engine, all of these being developed from the basic VW air cooled engine. Sadly Dr Ferdinand Porsche died in 1952, but his son, whose idea the 356 was, carried on with production.

Developments proceeded rapidly and many different body styles evolved from the Zuffenhausen works, while engine sizes increased gradually. By 1955 the 356A was available with a 1582cc 75 bhp engine, an engine that remained available right to the end of 356 production in early 1965, by which time it was producing 95 bhp at 5800 rpm. All sorts of body styles were available including a coupé, cabriolet, hardtop and the famous Speedster which had such a low soft top that visibility was severely impaired.

Something of a mystique grew up around the Porsche. Many drivers new to the car found the cornering abilities rather strange and many classed it as dangerous, but dedicated owners claimed that a special technique known as 'wischening' could be used on the steering and this eliminated any problems caused by the tendency of the swing axle rear suspension to allow the tail of the car to slide on corners. Certainly, the numbers of 356s still on the road seems to indicate that not too many were destroyed in accidents!

Almost from the beginning, Porsches took part in racing, rallies and record attempts, and their light weight more than made up for their lack of power. Over the years Porsche have won consistently in virtually every area of the sport except Formula 1.

The 356 remains as one of the great classics of modern motoring, and, although rust can attack the body and chassis, just as any other car, the Volkswagen-derived mechanical components allow it to be repaired quickly and relatively cheaply.

In Britain, 'Export or Die' was still the cry in 1949, and the Austin Motor Company took up the challenge by designing a car which they felt was tailored exactly for the American market. They had been exporting the Austin A40 Dorset and Devon to the USA for a couple of years with some success, although questionable reliability and the use of poor quality steel soon led to their demise. The car chosen for the American treatment was the A90, a fairly conventional car powered by a 2660cc four-cylinder engine which gave 88 bhp at 4400 rpm. This was simply a bored out version of the old Austin 16 engine but it endowed the Atlantic with a top speed of 90 mph and was later to form the power unit for the Austin Healey 100.

Mechanically, the car was quite conventional, with a live axle on leaf springs at the rear and independent front suspension. It was in the bodywork where the Atlantic differed from rather stodgy Austin tradition. At the front, the conventional radiator grille disappeared to be replaced by a narrow slatted grille, in the centre of which was a central 'Cyclops' spotlamp. The two main headlamps were faired into the front wings and the front wing line sloped downwards right to the rear bumper, the rear wheels being covered with small spats. A wide chrome-plated stripe swept down the centre of the bonnet. A convertible was announced first, and naturally, since it was destined for the American market, power operation of the soft top was available. A hardtop version followed in September 1949 and this remained in production until December 1952, whereas the convertible was dropped in late 1950.

Austin had seriously misjudged the American market, for they had plenty of American-looking cars of their own, much more garish than the Austin, much more powerful, and cheaper too. Despite successfully attacking American speed records at Indianapolis the A90 never really caught on. The car was put on sale in England where it did moderately well, but its poor fuel consumption in a time of austerity soon depressed sales to a trickle.

Although it has few of the attributes many

drivers demand of a classic car, the A90 Atlantic remains as a living testimony to an age when a company would do almost anything to attract foreign currency.

Another attempt to break into the American market was made with the Austin A40 Sports. This used the chassis of the A40 saloon with the power of the 1200cc engine increased from 40 to 46 bhp by the use of twin SU carburettors and larger inlet valves. The bodywork was built by Jensen of West Bromwich and the four-seater convertible looked very much like the then current Jensen Interceptor. It was quite a pretty car and was capable of 80 mph, together with a fuel consumption of 30 mpg, but although it continued until May 1953 not many were sold and those that remain are certainly collector's items.

Another Great British sporting name was that of Lea-Francis, but sadly its cars were too expensive for post-war times. This is one of the last cars, a 2½-litre 87 bhp sports model.

THE 1950's

A 1954 example of Bentley's attractive R-type Continental, known as the Flying Spur.

THE 1950S — EXPORT OR DIE

It might have been thought that five years after the end of the war the world would have recovered from the mauling it had taken, but in many countries restrictions were legion. In Britain food rationing was still in force, petrol was in short supply and of poor quality and even clothing was rationed. Taxation was punitive and imports were tightly restricted.

One man who was affected by import controls was Sydney Allard, who had been building 'specials' using the side valve Ford V8 engine from the British-built Ford Pilot for many years. When the Pilot engine went out of production he stockpiled a number of engines but he had to look round for an alternative, equally powerful engine. This was available in the USA in the shape of a new overhead valve Cadillac V8, but he could not import them in sufficient quantity; so he hit upon the idea of exporting his cars to the States minus engine and gearbox for American owners to fit their own.

The Allard was built in a small factory in Clapham, South London and each one was hand-built by a small team of mechanics. A multiplicity of models was produced and hardly two Allards are alike. He produced four-seater tourers, two-seater roadsters, two-door saloons, two-door coupés as well as out-and-out sports racing cars.

Undoubtedly the most famous Allard of all was the J2X. It began life for the 1950 season as the J2, a very simple two-seater sports car. It had a massive tubular steel chassis with a de Dion rear axle and front suspension by Allard's unique independent system which was achieved by cutting a Ford rigid front axle in half and mounting the inner ends on the chassis, thus giving swing axle front suspension. Drum brakes with shoes of 12-in diameter were fitted all round. The chassis was clothed in a doorless aluminium shell having cycle type front wings and small aero screens for the hardy driver.

The 'standard' engine was the side valve Mercury V8 of 4375cc capacity which gave about 110 bhp, but owners could also specify the overhead valve (ohv) conversion which had been developed by Zora Arkus-Duntov who later designed the Chevrolet Corvette. These light alloy heads pushed power up to 140 bhp and with a dry weight of only $18\frac{1}{2}$ cwt the J2 in this form was very fast indeed – in fact it could be too fast for its brakes.

The engineless cars were exported to the USA where the 180 bhp Cadillac unit was fitted, boosting top speed to 130 mph, from the 110 available with the ohv Mercury engine. This sort of performance was good enough to win races in the fledgling Sports Car Club of America races and for several years the Allard was *the* car to have in the States. Tom Cole was one of the most successful drivers and in 1950 he came to Europe to partner Sydney Allard to third place in the Le Mans 24 hour race. In 1952 Allard won the Monte Carlo rally in a P1 saloon with a Mercury engine. This was remarkable enough in itself, but Allard had been shot in the left eye with an airgun in his youth and had very little sight in that eye – a fact he somehow managed to conceal from the medical staff at race meetings.

The J2 was evolved into the J2X in 1951. This car had the engine placed $7\frac{1}{2}$ inches further forward in the chassis, the front suspension had radius arms located ahead of the axle and the nose of the car was extended further forward by about 6 inches. With a variety of engines such as Cadillac, Chevrolet, Lincoln and Chrysler, the J2X remained popular for a year or two, but the arrival of the XK120 and the later TR2 and Austin Healey 100 killed off its market as a road car because it was so much cruder and more expensive, while specialised sports/racing cars such as the C-type Jaguar and various Ferrari models ended Allards reign on the circuits.

By 1956 Allards were all but out of production, but anyone who has driven a J2 or J2X in anger will know something of the hairy chested days of sports car motoring.

For those whose definition of a classic car is a vehicle that is large, expensive and rare, practically every Bentley model must be included.

After the war Bentley restarted production with the Mk VI which was available with a standard steel body although coachbuilt versions were also available. The chassis was very similar to that of the Rolls-Royce Silver Wraith, since Rolls-Royce had owned the Bentley company since 1931. The massive separate steel chassis had a live rear exle mounted on leaf springs, and the independent front suspension was by double wishbones and coil springs. The power unit was a 4.2-litre six-cylinder featuring overhead inlet

Sidney Allard in the J2 with which he took third place at Le Mans in 1950.

valves and side exhaust valves. The Bentley version was fitted with twin SU carburettors whereas the Wraith had a single Stromberg. Despite its 16-ft length and 35¾-cwt dry weight the Mk VI could easily top 90 mph, even if acceleration was stately. Naturally it was trimmed with the best wood and leather that money could buy.

In 1951 the engine was increased in capacity to 4566cc by increasing the bore from 88.89 mm to 92 mm with a stroke remaining at 114.3 mm. Rolls-Royce refuse to release power output figures for their cars, allegedly replying by telegram to one enquiring customer who wanted to know the power output of his new car, with the single word 'sufficient'. Independent tests have revealed that the 4.2 six gave around 125 bhp and the 4.5-litre around 140 bhp. This was sufficient

to propel the 1951 Mk VI at a genuine 100 mph.

In 1952 the Mk VI gave way to the R-type Bentley which was mechanically similar apart from a slight increase in power, but a less angular body was fitted with a more gently sloping tail and improved boot space.

The most stunning Bentley of the time though was the Continental, which was built on the R-type chassis. This was a longer, lower and wider four-seater coupé with aluminium panelled bodywork by H. J. Mulliner. This two-door car with elegant rear wings and sloping fastback tail is regarded as perhaps the most attractive of the Continental variations that followed. The com-

pression ratio was increased to 7.25:1, improving power still further, and as its name implies it was able to cruise on the Continent at a steady 115 mph, yet this massive 2-ton car could still give 20 mpg.

In 1954 the bore was increased again, this time to 95.25 mm, to give a capacity of 4887cc and as an alternative to the four-speed gearbox with right-hand change the owner could specify the GM Hydramatic four-speed automatic transmission.

The Mulliner Continental was a very expensive car for the 1950s, for it cost more than £7000, but a good one will today fetch more than three times that figure. Later Continentals with the V8 engine were faster and more refined but to most Bentley *aficianados* the R-type Continental is

Probably the most famous of Donald Healey's early cars was the 2.4-litre Silverstone, one of which is seen here in 1950.

indisputably the best.

Donald Healey was a well known rally and racing driver before the war. As soon as the war finished he decided to build his own car, and for a number of years he built small numbers of specialised open two-seaters and sports saloons using the 2.4-litre Riley engine. Perhaps the most famous of these was the Healey Silverstone, a cycle-winged two-seater which set a number of young drivers on their racing careers, notably Tony Brooks, who later came close to winning the World Drivers' Championship. A later

variant was the Nash-Healey which was destined for export to the USA. Basically, it used the Healey Silverstone chassis but was fitted with the 3.8-litre overhead valve Nash six-cylinder engine which gave 130 bhp and endowed the rather slab sided roadster with a top speed of over 100 mph. This model was built from 1950 until 1952; then the car was fitted with the 4.1-litre version of the engine which gave 135 bhp, and this version remained in production until 1954. Healey's premises at Warwick were not geared for mass production and only just over 500 Nash-Healeys were sold in the States, largely because the car was more expensive than the much more exotic Jaguar XK120.

Salvation for Healey came at the 1952 London Motor Show. In an effort to find a car that would

The announcement of the Healey 100 in 1952 caused such a sensation that Healey could not hope to meet demand. Austin stepped in to manufacture the car, which was then called the Austin-Healey 100. This is a 100/4 of 1953 vintage competing at Goodwood, with racing screen.

sell in larger numbers than their previous models Donald Healey came up with a new ladder type chassis, underslung at the rear, with a live rear axle on leaf springs and wishbone coil spring independent front suspension. Into this he fitted the 2660cc four-cylinder engine from the Austin A90 Atlantic and a four-speed gearbox with centre floor change. This low projectile was clothed with a sleek all-enveloping body and was

fitted with a windscreen which could be removed and replaced at a shallower angle for high speed driving.

The car was the sensation of the 1952 Show and orders poured in at a price of around £1200, but the small Healey works had no hope of meeting these orders. Fortunately, Austin were looking for a new sporting car and when Sir Leonard Lord saw the Healey 100 he offered to take over manufacture. It was renamed the Austin-Healey 100 and production transferred to the Austin works at Longbridge, Birmingham.

The first twenty cars were built at the Healey works and serious production began in mid-1953. The specification had altered slightly, as the disc wheels were ditched in favour of more sporty wire wheels and the four-speed gearbox was dropped in favour of a three-speed gearbox with Laycock de Normanville overdrive.

The Austin-Healey 100/6 of 1956 had a smoother, six-cylinder, engine and could be had with an occasional rear seat.

The 90 bhp A90 engine had no great reputation for smoothness but it would slog the car up to a top speed of 100 mph quite easily, and with the screen lowered to the go-faster position it would reach 107 mph. The young bloods of the day loved to tear around in their Healeys, and the car was enormously successful in the USA where it soon began to make its mark in production sports car racing. In the States it sold for a modest $2985.

Donald Healey, relieved of the day-to-day task of building the cars, concentrated on developing faster versions as well as supervising record breaking and racing preparation. For the American market there was the 100M, a hotted-up 110 bhp version with an anti-roll bar at the front and improved handling, while the bonnet was fitted with louvres and a totally unnecessary leather strap, but at least it broadcast to all and sundry that this was an 'M' and not a common or garden variety.

In 1954 an even faster version, the 100S, was announced. This was loosely based on a very special car which had been driven to a speed of 192.6 mph on the Bonneville Salt Flats by Donald Healey. Harry Weslake developed a new light alloy cylinder head and together with numerous modifications to the crankshaft, camshaft, valves, lubrication and cooling, this engine pushed out 132 bhp at 4700 rpm. It was mated to a special four-speed close ratio gearbox, while body parts were in light alloy, and Dunlop disc brakes were standard fitments. This car was extremely successful in sports car racing, especially in the States. Owners who used them on the roads had to take care as the low build left little ground clearance and small rocks or even gate-stops in driveways could knock a hole in the oil sump.

The increased power being extracted from the old four-cylinder engine accentuated its roughness and in 1956 the car was given the six-cylinder C-type BMC engine. This 2639cc unit developed 102 bhp, giving the new model, the 100/6, a top speed of over 100 mph, and much needed smoothness. The wheelbase was increased by a couple of inches and the designers somehow managed to squeeze in a couple of children's seats, but a two-seater version was also available. The new model was considerably heavier than the 100 and with disc wheels instead of wire it was obviously intended for a less sporting clientele. However, the engine was capable of much further tuning and the 100/6 soon began to make a name for itself in rallying where the factory team notched up some notable successes.

In America the success of imported sports cars had not gone unnoticed, but in a country where production runs are measured in millions rather than in hundreds there was little profit to be made out of small-scale production and as yet the sports car imports were still in quite tiny numbers. For instance, total production of the Austin-Healey 100 between 1952 and 1956 was a mere 14,500 – hardly worth pressing the production line button for in Detroit.

General Motors got around the problem of high tooling costs for steel-bodied cars by making the body of their new sporty car in glass fibre reinforced plastics. In 1954 this was quite revolutionary and they turned out nearly 4000 in the first year despite teething problems.

The new car was the Chevrolet Corvette. In original form it could hardly be called a sports car and it was really a two-seater roadster. A standard Chevrolet chassis frame was shortened and lowered slightly, retaining the wishbone and coil spring independent front suspension and live rear axle with Hotchkiss drive. Power came from Chevrolet's famous 'Stovebolt' six, a 3.9 litre four main bearing overhead valve engine which gave a fairly healthy 150 bhp. Strangely, it was mated to the Powerglide two-speed automatic gearbox which stifled the performance somewhat. However, it would still accelerate to 60 mph from rest in 11 seconds and go on to a top speed of 105 mph. The plastic bodywork was well made and the shape, with its wide 'dollar grin' air intake was quite pleasing. It certainly had the makings of a sports car and with Zora Arkus-Duntov of Allard fame as the guiding light it was destined for better things.

Better things came in 1956 when Chevrolet dropped their 4.3-litre (265 cu in) V8 into the car. This was mated to a three-speed manual gearbox, while a hardtop became optional. From then on the power race was on with a vengeance and by 1957 the engine size had risen to 4637cc, increasing to 5358cc by 1962. Power output was almost anything the buyer could afford, and certainly for a modest outlay 250 bhp was possible, which was good enough to give a 0–60 mph figure of 6 seconds and a top speed around 120 mph.

The engine had become rather too fast for the chassis or the brakes in 1962 and for the 1963 season the car was completely revised and renamed the Corvette Stingray. Although a separate steel chassis frame was retained the suspension was completely revised, with a new independent rear suspension having lower wishbones located by trailing arms and the drive shafts acting as upper locating arms, as on the E-type Jaguar. Springing was by transverse leaf spring. Front suspension retained double wishbones and coil springs, with an anti-roll bar, while drum brakes were retained on all four wheels.

The standard engine was the aforementioned 5358cc (327 cu in) V8, tuned to give 360 bhp at 6000 rpm. It was mated to a three-speed manual gearbox as standard but there was also the option of a four-speed manual or two-speed automatic.

Bodywork was entirely new although still in glass fibre and was available as a striking fixed head coupé or as a convertible. The coupé featured doors running into the roof section and a split rear windscreen, while the headlamps on both models retracted behind shutters.

This model was capable of accelerating to 60 mph in a mere 5.3 seconds or reaching a top speed of 150 mph, depending on which final drive ratio was fitted. This model appealed very much to sporting Americans and production soon stepped up to 20,000 a year. It was also very successful on the race track and was more than a match for the then new E-type Jaguar.

The Stingray was an exhilarating car to drive, for its sheer brute power was almost unmatched by any other car on the road at that time. The E-type Jaguar generally had a higher top speed but the Corvette could out-accelerate it quite comfortably and it had a better gearbox too, although brakes and steering were not in the same league as those of the Jaguar.

At the same time as Chevrolet were moving into the sports car market so were Ford. However, Ford decided not to go for an out-and-out sports car with their Thunderbird because of the low volume sales that could be expected. Their solution to the problem was to design what they called a 'personal' car and although it was only a two-seater it was much bigger than the Corvette, being nearly 15 feet long and tipping

The Chevrolet Corvette had a modest power output when it was introduced in 1954, but various engine changes meant that by 1962, when this car was built, the chassis was really not up to the job. The Corvette Stingray of 1963 had all-new suspension and new bodywork, which was steadily developed thereafter.

the scales at 28 cwt. The chassis was conventional, utilising a steel channel frame with a live rear axle and the latest ball joint independent front suspension. The standard engine fitted was the 4785cc (290 cu in) overhead valve V8 which gave around 195 bhp, but an optional 5.1-litre (312 cu in) engine was available.

Bodywork was taken mostly from the Ford Fairlane but most of the ornamentation was removed, leaving a very simple shape which appealed greatly to the American public, who were used to chrome-covered cars. With its spare wheel hung vertically behind the boot the Thunderbird convertible looked smart in any company, while the hardtop was also a pleasant looking car. It was not as fast as the Corvette and did not handle as well, but it was a good deal cheaper ($2700 against $3500) and it outsold the Corvette nearly 10 to 1.

Unfortunately, Ford could not resist the temptation to make the Thunderbird available to a wider audience and by 1957 it had developed into a blousy overweight four-seater convertible just like a dozen other American cars.

Those original models that remain are as sought after as any other post-war American car.

Another car that was to make a great impact on the sporting world made an inauspicious appearance at the 1952 Earls Court Show in London. This was the Triumph 20SR, which was developed into the TR2.

Triumph's efforts to re-enter the sports car scene had started much earlier and in 1950 they showed a prototype of a new sporting vehicle at the Earls Court Show. Called the TR-X this roadster had all-enveloping bodywork of stressed skin construction and power provided by the Standard Vanguard engine. The strangest aspect of the car though, was its mass of hydraulic, electrical and vacuum-operated gadgetry. Hydraulics were used to raise and lower the soft top, move the seats and even raise the side windows, while engine vacuum was used to raise the radio aerial. The headlamps were hidden

The original Ford Thunderbird was a good looking two-seater and was certainly different, but by 1957 the T'bird looked like many other fat four-seaters. This is an early example of 1954.

behind flaps which were raised electrically. This car was obviously far too complicated to make its mark as a cheap, efficient sports car and it was quickly abandoned.

After an abortive attempt to buy the design rights to the Morgan Plus Four engineers went back to work to design a new car using existing components. Cobbled together in six months the 20SR prototype used a Standard Nine chassis, Triumph Mayflower front and rear suspension and the Standard Vanguard engine. Bodywork was stubby but attractive and public reaction was favourable, so the design was modified quickly and put on sale by March of 1953. The tail had been lengthened to provide some luggage room, and the engine, reduced in capacity to 1991cc, was tuned to give 90 bhp so that the then magic figure of 100 mph could be reached. In the then traditional way of proving the performance of British sports cars, Triumph's test driver Ken Richardson took a car fitted with an undertray and aero screen to the Jabbeke Highway near Brussels and recorded a top speed of 124 mph. The more prosaic production models were capable of exceeding 105 mph, and with a dry weight of under 18 cwt the car could accelerate to 60 mph in under 12 seconds, yet still record fuel consumption figures of 35 mpg.

The TR2 was an instant success both at home and abroad and the columns of motoring magazines around the world were full of letters from owners of TR2s and Austin Healey 100s, each proclaiming the merits of the particular car the writer happened to own. As far as competition was concerned the TR2 was more successful initially, taking first and second places on the 1954 RAC Rally, then going on to a host of race and rally successes.

The TR2 was not particularly sophisticated, but its rough engine was virtually unbreakable and although its handling in standard form was not exceptional it provided an excellent bridge between the rather outdated TF MG Midget of the time and the rather more 'pansy' all-enveloping Austin-Healey 100. With its cutaway doors the driver could hang his arm out in the fresh air and pretend that he was back in the pioneering days of motoring.

Like many other sports cars the TR2 grew more sophisticated and therefore heavier. A hardtop was available by late 1954 and the doors were shortened as it had been found that when parking next to high kerbs it was impossible to open the doors! The TR3 appeared in 1955 with 95 bhp available, which increased to 100 bhp in 1956. The TR3 also had the option of a tiny bench seat to fit behind the two main seats, but this gave sufficient leg room only for very small children.

The TR range evolved into the TR4 with completely new updated styling, then independent rear suspension followed on the TR4A and the final versions were the TR5 and TR6, fitted with the six-cylinder engine from the 2.5 PI saloon. By this time it had lost most of its pretensions of being a true sports car and the most eagerly sought after TRs are the TR2 and TR3, although the TR4 prior to the adoption of independent rear suspension is also highly regarded. The chassis frame was never really strong enough to take independent rear suspension and the crashing and banging when driving a TR4A, 5 or 6 on poor roads has to be experienced to be believed.

Britain's Rootes Group made a complicated range of cars after the war, largely because of acquisitions of other companies and by the mid-1950s the company made Hillman, Humber, Singer, Sunbeam and Sunbeam-Talbot cars as well as Commer commercial vehicles. Most of these were fairly plebeian family cars but Sunbeam-Talbot cars were of a more sporting nature.

The firm's sporting line began with the 80 and 90 models which first appeared in 1948 and although these were rather heavy and not particularly powerful their tough construction enabled them to survive in long distance rallies where all out speed was not the most essential requirement. The Sunbeam-Talbot 90, with a four-cylinder 2267cc engine giving 77 bhp at 4100 rpm in standard form, was particularly successful and this inspired the company to build a new more sporting model, developed from the drophead coupé version of the 90. This car was

The Triumph TR2 of 1953 was simple and unsophisticated, but it performed very well and was a great success.

The Mark III version of Rootes's Sunbeam-Talbot 90, built in 1956.

named the Alpine after the successes of the 90 in the Alpine rally.

Announced in March 1953 the Alpine resembled the convertible 90 in most respects except that it had a heavily louvred bonnet, while the more cumbersome drophead hood was replaced by a simple soft top used in conjunction with detachable sidescreens. A slight increase in power to 80 bhp enabled the standard model to reach 100 mph and in the now almost obligatory visit to that busy Jabbeke Highway in Belgium, rally driver Sheila van Damm drove a specially prepared model with undertray, high rear axle ratio and aero screens at a speed of over 120 mph.

The Talbot part of the name was dropped for the Alpine because possible confusion with the French-built Lago Talbots, although that make soon disappeared from the market. In a strange quirk of fate the takeover of the Chrysler plant in

Britain (which in turn used to belong to the Rootes Group), by the Peugeot-Citroën Group, has resulted in the make being named Talbot. Since there is a Sunbeam model on sale it now becomes Talbot Sunbeam, a complete reversal of its name in the 1950s.

The Alpine immediately began to score in International rallies and in 1953 the Sunbeam team won four *Coupes des Alpes*, the cups presented for penalty free runs in the tough Alpine Rally. Racing driver Stirling Moss won a Gold Cup for finishing three consecutive Alpine Rallies without incurring penalties and Sheila van Damm won the *Coupe des Dames* in the Alpine and also won the European Ladies

Championship.

For a long spell most Alpines were exported to the USA and few were ever made available for the home market. In 1954 overdrive became standard equipment on the Alpine although, strangely the car always retained a steering column gear change. However, many were converted to central floor change.

Despite its successes in rallies sales of the Alpine were never very high because it belonged to an outmoded period. The younger drivers could buy TR2s, Austin-Healey 100s, MGs and Morgans at much lower prices. Since several of these had better performance and more miserly fuel consumption than the big Alpine it quietly faded away at the end of 1955 and the Rootes Group retired from the sporting scene for a few years.

In 1953 yet another British sports car appeared

The sporting Sunbeam Alpine was developed from the Talbot 90 drophead and offered 100 mph performance. This is one of the 1954 works team cars.

on the roads. This was the AC Ace, made by the little firm in Thames Ditton whose factory was thoroughly steeped in motoring history. Like so many subsequent AC models the Ace happened almost by accident, but for all that it was one of the highlights of the 1953 London Show because it was the first all-British sports car to feature all-independent suspension and it was also one of the best looking sports cars to appear for some considerable time. Prior to building the Ace, the company had been building worthy if rather stuffy saloons and tourers, although before the war their previous Ace model was much sought after.

1959 AC Aceca, the beautiful sister car to the Ace. The Bristol 2-litre engine gave it a top speed of around 128 mph. Only 400 were built.

The Alvis TD21 replaced the TC21 in 1959 and was equipped with a 120 bhp engine and Mulliner coachwork to Graber design.

The Ace was really the brainchild of John Tojeiro, who designed and built racing cars at his small works in Royston, Hertfordshire. For a couple of seasons he had been running neat MG and Bristol engined sports/racing cars using a body shape very reminiscent of the Ferrari 166 sports car. The AC directors felt that this would make a good basis for a road car and John Tojeiro assisted with the conversion of his racing design to road use. The Ace used a massive twin tube chassis frame liberally cross braced and fitted with bracing hoops to strengthen the scuttle and rear bulkhead areas. At the front, suspension was by lower wishbones and a transverse leaf spring while rear suspension was very similar, the final drive unit being mounted on the chassis. Braking was by large finned $11\frac{3}{4}$ in drums all round and centre lock wire wheels were fitted. The body needed very little modification for road use and it was made from aluminium over a thin tube frame.

Power for the Ace came from the venerable six-cylinder two-litre overhead camshaft engine which AC had been making since 1919. Despite its age it responded to a little more tuning and yielded 85 bhp at 4500 rpm. Since the car's dry weight was only 15 cwt the engine was able to propel it to a top speed of 103 mph. A few changes were made before the Ace went into full production in 1954 including, regrettably, replacing the rack and pinion steering by one of the cam and peg type.

The Ace was well ahead of its time because the independent rear suspension endowed it with roadholding much superior to its rigid axled rivals. It was dearer than the TR2s and Austin-Healeys but it was undeniably better in most respects. However, the little firm tended to live in the past and they did not try to capitalise on the success of the Ace and never built them in sufficient numbers. Few dealers sold ACs and for most owners it was necessary to visit the factory to take a test drive, which was always arranged with exaggerated old world courtesy. The Sales Manager would conduct the car out to the Portsmouth Road where he handed over to the prospective customer. A coupé version of the Ace, the Aceca, followed in 1954 but this was not as successful as the open car although it was quite handsome in its own right. The noise level inside the coupé was quite high and it simply did not have the *cachet* of the open car.

With their increased production AC could not keep up with production of the engine as well as the complete car, so they began looking for an alternative. They settled on the Bristol 2-litre engine, which gave 105 bhp in touring form or 120 bhp if the competition engine was specified. This model was introduced in 1956 and the car was known as the Ace-Bristol. In 120 bhp trim it was good for 115 mph and a 0–60 mph acceleration time of 9.0 seconds. This made it very popular in 2-litre sports car racing and it won virtually everything open to it both in Britain and the USA. The factory made occasional forays into racing and in 1957 a front disc braked version finished second in the two litre class at Le Mans.

One of the most successful British AC drivers and dealers, Ken Rudd, decided to fit a less expensive engine into the Ace and he chose the 2.6 litre Ford Zodiac six-cylinder engine, which gave a modest 85 bhp in standard form, but various stages of tune were offered and this proved a popular choice with owners as it was some £500 cheaper than the Bristol engined car and spare parts were also considerably cheaper. This model continued alongside the Bristol engined versions until 1963, at which time AC had rather more pressing problems to deal with, as will be related in Chapter 3.

Of the British quality car makers perhaps Alvis were in the worst position at the end of the war as their factory had suffered severe damage and they survived on modified versions of their pre-war 12–70 model known as the TA and TB14, but in 1950 these were replaced by the brand new 3-litre TA21 model. This handsome new model evoked admiration right from the start. It featured a massive channel section chassis with six cross members and a new design of front suspension by double wishbones and coil springs. At the rear the live axle was mounted on semi-elliptic leaf springs. Braking was by two leading shoe drums, and wire wheels were fitted.

The new engine for the 3-litre had a bore and stroke of 84 mm × 90 mm giving a capacity of 2993cc. On a compression ratio of 7:1 and twin SU carburettors this six-cylinder engine gave 83

bhp at 4000 rpm. It was a very strong unit, with a seven main bearing crankshaft and over the years it was tuned to give greatly increased power outputs.

Three models were available initially, a four-door saloon, a two-door drophead coupé and the TB21, a two-seater sports tourer with a body based on that of the TB14. This was not very popular and was soon dropped.

Power output was soon raised to 95 bhp which increased the top speed to over 90 mph, and the car enjoyed steady demand from a well-heeled clientele, one of whom was the Duke of Edinburgh, who kept his 3-litre long after the factory had closed down.

Alvis had considerable problems with supplies of bodies because Tickford, who built the drophead coupé, was taken over by Aston Martin who needed the facilities for their own bodies, while Mulliners of Birmingham, who made most of the Alvis bodywork, were taken over by Standard-Triumph. Alvis solved the problem by going to Swiss coachbuilder Graber of Berne who had been building special bodies on Alvis chassis for some years. He supplied bodies until an agreement was reached with Park Ward of London to build the Graber design under licence.

By this time the TC21/100 Grey Lady model which had been on the market for a couple of years incorporated a number of improvements, not least of which was a power increase to 100 bhp at 4000 rpm which enabled the car to reach 100 mph.

Further improvements were made to the car over the years and power increased to 150 bhp, but demand for Alvis cars was low. In 1965 Rover took over the company, but they themselves shortly joined British Leyland, and in 1967 the last Alvis car was built. It was one of the last true coachbuilt cars in series production when it went out of production.

One of the greatest and most desirable of all classic cars burst on a startled motoring world in 1954. This was the Mercedes-Benz 300SL, a car that was as far ahead in its time as the XK120 Jaguar had been in 1948. But Mercedes had the disadvantage of working in a virtually destroyed factory for several years and then toiling under the direction of the occupation forces until

The Mercedes-Benz 300SL was a true classic. Its
multi-tube spaceframe chassis gave away its racing
heritage and its gull-wing doors gave it a very
distinctive style. This is a 1956 version.

The MGA coupé followed the convertible into production in 1956. It was slightly quicker than the open car, having a little more power.

restrictions were lifted in the early 1950s.

The 300SL began life as a racing car in 1952. Powered by a six-cylinder engine developed from the roadgoing 220 and 300 engines the seven main bearing unit gave 175 bhp from its 3 litres. Fitted in a lightweight aluminium bodied coupé with gull wing doors this all independent suspension machine was technically way ahead of the opposition in 1952. They won at Le Mans, Nürburgring, Berne and the Carrera PanAmerica plus second place in the Mille Miglia.

Having proved their point Mercedes began perfecting the 300SL for road use and the new car appeared in 1954. The chassis of the 300SL was a pure space frame, with numerous small diameter tubes giving the chassis its strength. Because of the height of the chassis it could not have conventional doors so the gull wing arrangement was retained for the road car. The power unit had undergone considerable development and the 2996cc six now yielded 240 bhp at 6000 rpm

using Bosch fuel injection and dry sump lubrication. Front suspension was by wishbones and coil springs while rear suspension used swing axles. Braking was by heavily finned drum brakes all round and steering was by recirculating ball.

By the standards of the day the 300SL was sensational. Not only did it look like something from outer space it went like it too. It comfortably reached a top speed of 130 mph and could accelerate to 60 mph in under 7 seconds, performance which only very specialised sports cars could match.

Not that the 300SL was perfect. Its swing axle rear end would slide very easily, especially in the wet and the drum brakes could fade if an enthusiastic driver punished them. It was a very expensive car too, costing about £4500 in Britain

In 1955, which would buy a Rolls Royce Silver
Cloud or a very big house! Because the engine
was canted over to the left it meant that the car
could not be made available in right-hand drive.
In any case most of the 1400 car production went
to the USA.

Mercedes recognised that the high sills restricted sales to less agile customers, so the car
was re-designed for 1957 with much lower
chassis sides, so that a normal two-door roadster
body could be fitted. This proved more popular
than the gull wing version.

For the less wealthy, Mercedes produced the
190SL with a four-cylinder 120 bhp engine.
Although it looked much like the 300SL roadster
it had nowhere near the performance and sold to
those who wanted a comfortable two-seater for
fast touring. It stayed in production until 1962
long after the 300SL had disappeared.

In Italy Alfa Romeo had been building cars in
relatively small quantities since the war despite

*The MGA Twin Cam had all the hallmarks of a
fine car, with disc brakes all round and a new 108
bhp power unit. However, the engine was somewhat
fragile and only about 2000 cars were built between
1958 and 1960.*

their total domination of Grand Prix racing.
However, in 1955 they announced a completely
new car which captured the imagination of
enthusiasts the world over and set Alfa Romeo on
the road to recovery. This was the Giulietta
Sprint Veloce, a little jewel of a car that had
enthusiasts slavering at the mouth. It was an
exquisite tiny coupé styled by Bertone which
looked right from every angle, and still does for
that matter.

Mechanically, the Giulietta was based on the
bigger 1900 model which remained in production. The twin overhead camshaft engine of
the 1900 was scaled down, with a bore and stroke

of 74 mm × 75 mm to give a capacity of 1290cc. Even in mildly tuned single carburettor form this all alloy engine gave 60 bhp at 5500 rpm. Front suspension was by double wishbones and coil springs while a live rear axle was retained, as on the 1900. At a price little more than half that of the 1900 Italians flocked to buy the little coupé and the factory was kept busy for years coping with the demand. Although the engine was small it would rev its heart out and the roadholding was an Italian driver's dream. It soon became popular with racing drivers and it was a perennial class winner. Some six months after the coupé was announced a four-door saloon, the Berline arrived, then a stretched limousine version and finally the very attractive looking Pininfarina bodied Spider two-seater open car which somehow managed to retain the lines of the coupé yet looked attractive in its own right.

The original Sprint Veloce would do an easy 105 mph on its 60 bhp, but later models went even faster as power climbed to 90 bhp at 6500 rpm, while the competition Giulietta SS with 100 bhp would top 120 mph. All this from 1290cc!

The Giulietta carried on until 1962, at which time 157,000 examples had been built. Sadly, rust has depleted their numbers badly but anyone lucky enough to find one today will find that it is still a little jewel of a car.

The famous twin-cam engine lives on in the Giulia, Alfetta and the new Giulietta, but none of the modern Alfas can evoke the enthusiasm of keen drivers like those little Giuliettas of the 1950s.

By 1955 it was obvious that MG's TF model was hopelessly out of date, as only Morgan could get away with body designs that dated from the 1930s. The Austin Healey and TR2 had stolen MG's market in the States and although MG and Austin-Healey were in the same firm by then, there was still intense rivalry.

The way that MG would go was indicated to the perceptive by a car that ran in the 1951 Le Mans race. Entered by a private owner George Phillips, who was photographer to Autosport magazine this special bodied TD was very reminiscent of the eventual MGA which appeared in 1955. Although this was a private venture, MGs designer Syd Enever designed the body and had the car built at the MG factory. He

also kept a watching brief on the car and was impressed by the speed of the car because it slipped through the air so much easier than the angular MGs, even the TF which had its radiator grille tilted backwards.

MG carried out much of their development through racing and record breaking and the next step in the MGA story was the EX 179 a record-breaking car which was taken to the Bonneville Salt Flats where it secured class records in the hands of George Eyston and Ken Miles at speeds up to 153.69 mph. The engine of this car was the old MG unit with a new block which gave a capacity of 1466cc but this engine was due to die when the MG TF went out of production and the next step was to fit a new engine, the BMC 'B' series unit, into a team of cars which would run in the 1955 Le Mans race. Although only mildly tuned to give 84 bhp two of the cars ran steadily in the race to finish 5th and 6th in their class and 12th and 17th overall, a very creditable performance, for the chassis was very much like that of the MGA although the bodywork was of aluminium instead of steel. This car, the EX 182, formed the basis of the production MGA which was announced in September 1955.

With its sleek all-enveloping bodywork the MGA was an immediate success both at home and abroad. Although it was pretty conventional even by the standards of 1955 it did not have the slabsided look of the Austin-Healey 100 yet was not as ugly as the TR2. MG enthusiasts who had turned up their noses at the old fashioned MG TF flocked to buy the MGA and over 13,000 were built during 1956.

With coil spring and wishbone front suspension and a live rear axle on semi-elliptic leaf springs it was not exceptional in any way but it handled better than the TR2 and with the 'B' series 1489cc engine tuned to give 68 bhp at 5500 rpm it had a top speed of 96 mph.

In 1956 the open two seater was joined by a pretty, fixed head coupé version which was even quicker than the open car. Power output had been raised to 72 bhp at 5500 rpm and the coupé would reach 103 mph.

MG were not content with the pushrod 'B' series car and in July 1958 they announced the MGA Twin Cam, a new twin overhead camshaft engine with a capacity of 1588cc and a power

A 1951 example of the Pegaso Z102, equipped with a factory-built body.

output of 108 bhp at 6700 rpm. The chassis into which it was fitted was similar to that of the MGA except that Dunlop disc brakes were fitted on all four wheels and handsome centre-lock disc wheels were standard.

The Twin Cam would accelerate to 60 mph in a splendid 9 seconds and had a top speed of 115 mph, which brought forth a torrent of praise from the motoring press. Unfortunately, the Twin Cam did not continue giving this performance for very long and owners were soon breaking down with monotonous regularity. I experienced this myself when testing a works car for a magazine. It seemed to consume a lot of oil in the first two or three days I had the car, but was undeniably rapid. Unfortunately, a clatter from the engine when starting up one morning signalled the end of the test, as a valve had 'dropped'. It was towed away ignominiously and it never came back for re-test.

MG blamed twin cam engine failures on unsympathetic drivers who over-revved the engine or used unsuitable fuel but the truth was that the engine was not really suitable for road use in the same way as Jaguar's twin cam engine. Sadly, production of the Twin Cam stopped in April 1960 and the remaining disc braked chassis were used up by fitting the pushrod engine from the ordinary MGA. Only 2000 odd Twin Cams were produced and those that remain are undoubtedly classics.

Spain had suffered first from her civil war then from being cut off from the rest of Europe during World War II, which resulted in her motor industry developing painfully slowly. It was really only when the Fiat-backed SEAT factory got under way in the 1950s that new cars began to be built in any quantity.

It was in this strange climate that the Pegaso commercial vehicle works suddenly decided to build a sports car of exotic specification and so expensive that few in its native country could hope to afford one. The inspiration for this car came from the chief designer of the parent company ENASA, Wilfredo Ricart, who had spent some years as a designer with Alfa Romeo, while the motive behind the new car was said to be a desire to train apprentices thoroughly.

The engine for the first sports car was a water-cooled V8 with twin overhead camshafts per bank, having a bore and stroke of 75 mm × 70 mm for a capacity of 2474cc. With a sturdy five bearing crankshaft, dry sump lubrication and running on a modest 7.5:1 compression ratio the engine developed 170 bhp at 6300 rpm using a single Weber carburettor. But with more carburettors and high compression ratios the engine power increased to 225 bhp.

The car into which this engine was fitted was the Z102, which itself was quite advanced. Front suspension was by double wishbones and torsion bars while at the rear a de Dion tube axle was utilised. The five speed gearbox was mounted in unit with the final drive at the rear of the car and braking was by massive 14-in Lockheed drum brakes.

A variety of bodies were available on the Z102, including open two-seaters and pretty two-door coupés, many of them provided by foreign coachbuilders such as Touring of Milan. This firm produced a strangely prophetic coupé in 1953 which featured rear-mounted aerofoils running from the roof down to the bodywork on each side of the car.

Engine size increased gradually, first to 2.8 litres then to 3.2, by which time 280 bhp was being claimed. A supercharged two-seater was timed over the flying mile at 152 mph in 1953 and in the same year a pair of special cars were entered for the Le Mans 24 Hour race. Unfortunately one car crashed in practice, killing its driver and the other was withdrawn.

The standard Z102 coupé was certainly good for 125 mph and although buyers had to pay anything up to £5000 for the car in the 1950s they were assured of a three-year guarantee and any modifications made to the car at a later date were all allegedly done free of charge.

A new model, the Z103, was announced in 1956. This had a less exotic engine, being a

pushrod ohv V8 with capacities ranging from 4 to 4.7 litres. Power outputs as high as 330 bhp, with top speeds in excess of 150 mph, were quoted for this car but few people had the opportunity to find out as only four were made and in 1958 the firm retired from car making to go back to making trucks and buses, which they still do today. Only about 125 Pegasos were made and, for that reason alone, any that come onto the market will command an astronomical price.

BMW were in a worse state than Mercedes at the end of the war, for their plant at Eisenach fell in the Russian sector and it soon retired behind the Iron Curtain, where BMW look-alikes called EMWs were built. However, BMW had a motorcycle factory in Munich and after many problems they returned to car production with the 501 powered by the pre-war six-cylinder 2-litre engine. They decided that their future did not lie in mass production and in 1954 a new V8 engine appeared. This 2.6-litre all alloy V8 was introduced at the 1954 Geneva Motor Show, and although the 502 model in which it was fitted was merely the bulbous 501 with the new engine it created a favourable impression. With 100 bhp available it would just about exceed 100 mph and it began to appeal to a small but discerning

clientele. They scaled up the engine to 3168cc and a power output of 140 bhp at 4800 rpm for the 503 model, but their *pièce de resistance* was a two seater roadster which became available in 1955 with the 3.2-litre engine. This car, the 507 was a very pretty all-enveloping two-seater sports car which was capable of a top speed of 150 mph from the V8, which in 507 form had an increase in compression ratio and a power output of 150 bhp.

Unfortunately it appeared at the same time as the Mercedes-Benz 300SL and was also very expensive. Those who wanted high performance could buy a much cheaper Jaguar and those who wanted exclusivity could have a 300SL. As a result only 250 were built in four years. But those 250 are as sought after today as any other classic.

In 1954 the vintage looking Citroën 6in front wheel drive car was given hydropneumatic rear suspension. Few people gave this much thought,

dismissing it as yet another gimmick to try to keep an ageing car afloat – after all the shape of the Six dated from the 1930s.

But in 1955 Citroën shook the world with the announcement of the most technically advanced saloon car that had yet been seen. This was the DS19, which was different in almost every respect from its contemporaries. The first shock was its appearance, for its nose disappeared to a point and there seemed to be no way in for the cooling air. At the rear the bodywork sloped almost to the bumper and the rear wheels were totally enclosed by the bodywork.

The suspension of the car was revolutionary, as the all-independent suspension was by oleo-pneumatic struts, fed from a central reservoir and a pump which was driven by a belt from the engine. At the end of a journey the suspension settled gently and when the engine was started it would gently pump itself up to the correct ride

Although only a few were built, BMW's 507 was a fine car. It had a top speed of 130 mph and was well styled, but it was too expensive.

height irrespective of how much weight was carried. It kept the body level no matter how weight changed or how bad the roads were.

Nor was this the end of the surprises for the steering was power-assisted, the clutch was operated pneumatically, the brakes were power-operated too, by a tiny button on the floor, and the car could be jacked up by using the oleo-pneumatic suspension to do the work for you.

To start the DS (Déesse or Goddess) the driver simply pushed the column mounted gear lever towards the centre of the car. This started the engine and then all the driver had to do was push the gear lever into the gear required, the automatic clutch mechanism operating the clutch.

One familiar feature of the DS was the engine, for the old four-cylinder 1911cc engine had been

Citröen took the world by storm with their DS19 in 1955. Just about every system was more advanced than ever before.

retained, although improved combustion chamber shape and a different camshaft had boosted power to 63 bhp, giving the car a top speed of 85 mph. The engine was perhaps the one major disappointment of the car because such a futuristic car needed a modern engine and the most favourable comment that journalists made about it was that it was 'agricultural'.

Many drivers found the unconventional controls rather distracting and the DS needed a lengthy period of acclimatisation before a driver could extract the best from it. It was easy to crash the gears by moving the lever faster than the

This Tour de France coupé of 1958 was just one of a long series of Ferrari 250GT's. It was so named because such cars won the Tour de France in 1957, 1958 and 1959.

automatic clutch could operate and the tiny button which passed for a brake pedal was easy to miss, so new drivers tended to stamp their foot around on the floor until they hit the button – the car would then stand on its nose because the button needed only the lightest caress to bring the car to a stop. Another first for the DS was that it was the first production car to use disc brakes on the front wheels, despite the long-held belief that Jaguar were first. Many drivers also distrusted the single spoke steering wheel, not believing that it could be strong enough.

Citröen bowed to public pressure in 1956 by introducing a much simplified version of the car, the ID19. This retained the oleo-pneumatic suspension but the braking system used a normal pedal and the gearbox returned to normal manual selection. The engine of this model was the older lower power unit but since it was lighter performance was much the same.

The DS and ID were always quite expensive and therefore never sold in large numbers, especially outside France where the car's ability to cover poorly surfaced roads at speed was not a priority. This ability gave the DS some remarkable successes in long distance rallies where durability was more necessary than speed. A brace of victories in the Monte Carlo rally, plus victories in the Tour of Corsica and the legendarily difficult Liege–Sofia–Liege rally showed the

One of the last of the Rolls-Royce Silver Cloud SII models, this car was built in 1962. However, the SIII was very little altered, the number of headlamps giving the external clue.

stamina of the car, while a heartbreaking accident short of the finish robbed Lucien Bianchi of victory in the London to Sydney Marathon race.

The DS and ID carried on in production in largely unchanged form except for increased power for over 20 years and they were only replaced by the CX range which continues to use the formula established in 1955. This is truly a classic car.

Rolls-Royce continued on their own sweet way throughout the 1950s, eschewing design innovations for their own sakes. A new piece of engineering had to be outstandingly superior to existing practice for it to be even considered, then it had to be extensively tested and modified. Even the General Motors Hydramatic automatic gearboxes used in Rolls-Royce and Bentley models were all dismantled, modified to suit Rolls-Royce, then rebuilt and tested before being fitted to a car.

So the new Silver Cloud model of April 1955 which replaced the Silver Dawn was really only an evolutionary model. The chassis was much the same, but the wishbone and coil spring front suspension was slightly modified and an anti-roll bar fitted. The old six-cylinder engine received a new six port head but otherwise the car was mechanically unchanged. The standard steel body of the Cloud was more subtly modern than that of its predecessors and it was warmly received by Rolls-Royce fanciers, although some people looked sideways at the Bentley S1 which was no more than a Rolls-Royce Silver Cloud fitted with a Bentley radiator and badges. Naturally, chassis were still available for the great coachbuilders like Park Ward, Mulliner and James Young to erect special bodies, and some delightful bodies they made too.

The next major step came with the Silver Cloud II of 1959 which was fitted with a brand new all aluminium V8 engine of 6.2-litre capacity. Naturally, accusations were made that the engine was copied from an American V8 but no

Ford's Edsel is probably the most famous motoring 'flop'. It cost the company nearly 350 million dollars before it was finally killed off in 1960. This example was made in 1959, just before the strange radiator grille was altered.

The Chrysler 300 series was one of the company's more successful products, spanning ten years from 1955 to 1965. This is the 300G model of 1961.

one could find any serious resemblance to existing units, and the whispering silence of the new V8 was its own reply to critics. The new engine gave the Cloud II a top speed of 115 mph and acceleration from 0–60 mph of around 10 seconds, which would leave many a sports car standing at the traffic lights. Then in 1962 Rolls-Royce created something of a furore by bringing out a Series 3 Silver Cloud and equivalent Bentley model. These were essentially unchanged but had been fitted with quadruple headlights. Rolls-Royce snobs argued that 'quad' lamps were alright for flashy American cars and 'cheap' cars like Jaguars but after all a Rolls was a Rolls and this sort of thing just was not done. Well, it had been done and Rolls-Royce were not about to change the design. In any case they knew that they had something else up their sleeve.

Ask anyone to name a classic car and the chances are he or she would say Ferrari. The combination of staggering speed, exotic bodywork invariably painted blood red, the prancing horse insignia and the thrilling experience of driving a car associated with so many racing victories is a spine tingling feeling for any enthusiast.

Ferrari had been building road cars ever since the late 1940s, but few of them could be considered as serious vehicles, since they often lacked creature comforts and hardly any two cars were the same, but Ferrari realised that a stable

road car range would provide finance for his motor racing programme, so in the early 1950s the 250 range was born.

The 250 stemmed from the 250 Mille Miglia model which used a 3.3-litre V12 engine with cylinders linered down to bring the capacity under 3 litres. This was intended for competition use but was not very successful (apart from Braco's famous victory over Mercedes in the 1952 Mille Miglia) so it was converted for road use and the first road car with the 250 designation was the 250 Export fitted with a V12 engine designed by Ing. Lampredi, which had a bore and stroke of 68 × 68 mm and a capacity of 2963cc. This single cam per bank V12 gave 220 bhp at 7000 rpm using triple Weber carburettors. This was replaced by the 250 Europa in 1953 which was basically similar, but the engine had been

The Lotus Elite of 1957 was Colin Chapman's first closed car. It was also the first car to utilise a glassfibre body/chassis unit. It set sports car handling/roadholding standards for many years. This car was built in 1961.

detuned for reliability reasons to give 200 bhp, while the old five-speed gearbox was replaced by a new four-speed unit.

This model remained in production for a couple of years but was replaced in 1955 by the 250GT. For this model the Lampredi-designed engine was replaced by the V12 engine designed by Ing. Columbo, dating back to the 125 model. With a bore and stroke of 73 mm × 58.8 mm this engine had a capacity of 2953cc, a compression ratio of 8.5:1 and with triple Weber 36DCZ

carburettors this engine gave 220 bhp at 7000 rpm, just like its predecessor. Power went via a multiple disc clutch to the four-speed gearbox which now had Porsche type baulk ring synchromesh.

Suspension was by wishbone and coil springs at the front in conjunction with Houdaille shock absorbers, while the lightweight live rear axle was hung on semi elliptic leaf springs. Two-leading shoe brakes were used on all four wheels and large 5 × 16-in wire wheels were used.

A variety of body builders had been used for the 250 range. The first bodies on the 250 chassis were mostly made by Touring of Milan but Vignale took over for a spell and then for the 250 Europas, PininFarina built most of the bodies. When Ferrari laid down a proper 'production line', building about one car a day, PininFarina built the coupé bodies, while the local body-builder Scaglietti did a convertible as well as building the competition car bodies.

The majority of bodies were built in aluminium and no unnecessary weight was added in the way of trim or soundproofing so the cars were very light and consequently fast. With suitable gearing the car could do 150 mph, but the early cars were happiest with a lower final drive for better acceleration and a top speed around the 130 mph mark, still quite enough to see off practically everything on the road.

I have been fortunate enough to drive a number of these fascinating V12 engined cars and I find them among the most satisfying of cars to drive. The early cars are the best to my mind because they are very simple – they just have the bare minimum of equipment necessary to conduct a car quickly around the countryside. The engine is very impressive because it is so untemperamental, unlike many exotic engines. It does not start quickly, but the metallic clang of the starter, followed by an impressive whirr of machinery is soon suppressed below the mellow burble of the engine bursting into life, the thrash of the camshaft chains just audible at idle. Once the engine is revved the intake roar of the Weber

The DB2 was the first of Aston Martin's 'modern' range of cars, being announced in 1950 with a twin-cam straight-six designed by W. O. Bentley.

carburettors is the dominant sound and the keen driver is lost in the wonder of that flexible yet powerful engine.

The gearbox may not be the most positive or fastest, but the satisfying clunk as each gear drops home is unmatched by any other gearbox. Just to accelerate up and down through the gears is satisfying enough, but to take a 250GT through a series of bends is perhaps one of the ultimate joys of motoring. Certainly, there are cars that can corner faster, but few of them will match that solid feel of being glued to the road.

So good was the basic 250GT that many owners raced them with success. The arduous Tour de France, a rally-cum-race, was a speciality with Ferrari drivers and a 250GT won it in 1957, 1958 and 1959, while it was also good enough to win the GT class in the 1957 Mille Miglia. The 250GT subsequently appeared in almost every race that was open to it and seldom had to give best to other makes in the GT class.

In 1959 Ferrari announced a new racing version of the 250GT, the Berlinetta, with lightweight bodywork by Scaglietti. The engine was tuned to give around 280 bhp and with a weight of under 19 cwt it would accelerate to 100 mph in under 12 seconds and with long gearing would exceed 160 mph. Quite a large number of these Berlinettas were built and they became outstandingly successful in racing. A steel-bodied version was also built for road use.

In 1960 came one of Ferraris rare failures. This was the 250GTE which was a 2 + 2 coupé with rather uninspiring Farina bodywork. The V12 engine gave 235 bhp and Laycock de Nomanville overdrive was fitted. Unfortunately the car was quite heavy by Ferrari standards and did not handle very well, while the overdrive did not take too kindly to the power output and failed quite frequently. However, it would still do 135 mph and was pleasant when used as a touring car.

In America the leviathan reigned supreme during the 1950s and although imports still had their small niche in the market, the foreign cars were still too small and cramped for the majority of home drivers.

In 1953 Ford were expanding rapidly and were planning to take another crack at General Motors who still had the biggest slice of the market. Many people inside the Ford company felt that

they needed another range of cars to give them a wider base on which to sell. Some felt that they needed a new high priced car under the Mercury name to sell against the more expensive Buicks and Oldsmobiles, but others felt that a completely new name was essential. The Lincoln Mercury division of Ford felt that the new car should be slightly more up market, selling at a higher price than the Mercury range. In their report on the proposed new model they referred to it as the Edsel, after Edsel Ford, who had died recently.

Finally, the company decided to appease both groups by proceeding with two new models, a cheaper car to sell against Dodge and Pontiac and a more expensive version to pit against Buick, de Soto and Oldsmobile.

After much discussion over *marque* names it was finally decided to name the car Edsel and in late 1957 they were revealed to the public. Technically the cars were quite advanced, with coil spring and wishbone front suspension, live rear axle on leaf springs, self adjusting drum brakes and a new automatic transmission with push buttons for gear selection. Two V8 engines were available, a 6 litre (360 cu in) and a 6.9 litre (410 cu in) and the choice of manual or automatic gearboxes was available.

The cheaper models were the Ranger and Pacer while the up-market versions were the Corsair and Citation. Bodywork was fairly orthodox American for the period except for the radiator grille, which was a tall 'horse's collar' contraption which even by the garish American standards of the time was thought to be strange. In addition, the car sales boom of 1954, when the car was dreamed up, had evaporated by 1957 and sales were nowhere near the expected levels. Also, the car tended to take sales away from Ford's Mercury range rather than rival makes.

In an attempt to bolster sales a cheaper version with a straight six engine was introduced, and in 1959 the bodywork was restyled, omitting the curious 'horse's collar'. But it was too late. The fickle public had lost interest in the Edsel and before 1960 dawned the Edsel operation was

The famous Aston-Martin twin-cam engine, seen here in a DB5.

wound up with losses approaching $350,000,000.

In the strange way that car collecting works, the worthy designs are often ignored while cars like the Edsel are gradually acquiring status and value as collectors' items. Since total Edsel sales were probably less than 200,000, which is minimal by American standards, and bearing in mind the high scrapping rate in the States, the Edsel is already a rarity.

General Motors, Ford and Chrysler made up America's big three after the war, but Chrysler were relegated to number three position right from the outset. After their disaster with the advanced Chrysler Airflow in the 1930s, Chrysler seldom essayed any technical advances for fear of a repetition of that traumatic period. Consequently the cars became rather stodgy and uninspired.

Things stayed that way until 1951. In that year Chrysler came out with an engine that was way ahead of anything else on the market in the USA. Until that time Chrysler had been making a straight eight, but the V8 that replaced it was not only 100 lb lighter it was much more compact and it was far more powerful. The original V8 had a capacity of 5.4 litres (331 cu in) and with hemispherical combustion chambers, double rocker arms and a generally very advanced specification it gave 180 bhp compared with the straight-eight's 135 bhp. This gave the top line Chrysler models a top speed of 100 mph, which naturally attracted the attention of young drivers. Chrysler were quick to seize on the sales potential of the powerful 'Fire Power' engine and Chryslers tended to be among the fastest of American cars.

In 1955 they announced the 300 range, which although designed as normal four-seater sedans and coupés were more powerful and faster than the Ford Thunderbird or Chevrolet Corvette. The 300 stood for the power output, which although inflated for publicity purposes, was still a lot of horsepower. Although the 300 was essentially a cut down New Yorker with a different rectangular radiator grille, it sold well,

The DB4 was considered by Aston fans to be the best of the post-war cars; DB5's such as this were thought to be overweight tourers.

simply because it could exceed 120 mph with ease, even though it weighed two tons.

For 1956 the engine was increased to 5.8 litres and the power claimed was now a hefty 355 bhp, which still kept the 300 well ahead of the opposition. The 1958 model, called the 300D now had an engine of 6423cc and a claimed power output of 380 bhp at 5200 rpm. They even offered a fuel-injected version of the engine as an option, with a power output nudging 400 bhp.

The horsepower race had to stop somewhere and the power ratings started to decrease somewhat after 1958. The 300 range carried on until 1965 with the 300L but they were never quite the same as those early 'Hemi's'.

Such was Chrysler's reputation as engine builders that many foreign car makers bought them for their quality cars, including Facel-Vega, Allard, Jensen and Bristol. In fact Bristol use them to this day.

Every generation seems to throw up a genius, and in Colin Chapman Britain found an engineering genius of unbelievable talent. Although he was not the first to use a multi-tubular space-frame chassis he certainly perfected it and his first production car, the Lotus 6, used this form of chassis in a doorless, cycle-winged two-seater which became popular with young enthusiasts who built up their cars from kits of parts. His racing cars used similar chassis and because of their light weight and superb roadholding they won innumerable races for small capacity cars. Chapman was ambitious though, and he wanted to expand his company into a front league car manufacturer. To achieve this meant abandoning the space frame chassis because this was time consuming to build, required a great deal of skilled labour and had severe limitations for a road car, as the height of the chassis side rails limited access.

He decided on a revolutionary solution. There was little chance of a small company being able to acquire the finance for tooling up for a steel monocoque body/chassis so he hit on the idea of a monocoque chassis made entirely from glass fibre reinforced plastics. The car was made from three main mouldings, a lower chassis section, which incorporated the few steel mounting points for suspension, etc., an inner tub section and the outer skin. The outer skin of this new car, the

Elite, was undoubtedly one of the prettiest and most practical ever seen on a small GT car. This glass fibre body/chassis unit proved to be very rigid as well as extremely light.

The power unit chosen for the car was the Coventry-Climax FWE, a single overhead camshaft 1216cc four-cylinder all-aluminium engine which produced 75 bhp at 6100 rpm. This engine started life as a portable fire pump engine, having been designed by a racing engine designer who had an eye for its eventual potential as a racing engine! In the Elite it was mated to a BMC 'B' series gearbox, drive being taken to a chassis mounted differential. Suspension was independent on all four wheels, by wishbones and coil springs at the front and by novel and simple Chapman struts at the rear, in which the drive shafts located the rear wheels, along with radius arms. Girling disc brakes were fitted on all four wheels and steering was by rack and pinion.

I first encountered the Elite at the Goodwood racing circuit and when I drove it I could not believe how fast it could corner, allied to beautifully light and accurate steering and very powerful brakes. Later experience on the road showed that some noise was transmitted through the monocoque shell from the wheels and ventilation was inefficient, but these were small prices to pay.

The car did not get into full production until 1959 and a year later a Mk II version was announced. This had improved interior trim and modified rear suspension, while a Special Equipment version was also offered. This had a slight increase in power to 83 bhp at 6500 rpm and the German-built ZF gearbox was standard equipment.

There were problems with the quality of glass fibre mouldings and a contract was given to the Bristol Aeroplane Company to build the bodies, and a marked improvement was found in these stronger body/chassis units.

Being a Lotus, the Elite was used in competition with great success and many class wins were notched up in international races such as the Nürburgring 1000 Kilometres and Le Mans 24 Hour race, as well as countless Club events. One of the most successful Elites was a car fitted with Hobbs Mechamatic automatic gearbox and raced by David Hobbs. I had the pleasure of driving this at Silverstone and still regard it as one of the most exciting and best handling GT cars I have ever driven.

Sadly, the Elite had to be dropped by Lotus in early 1964 after only 988 had been built. The chassis/body unit was very expensive to build and the nature of the design meant that a convertible version could not be designed, so it was abandoned in favour of the Elan model.

For another British specialist builder the post-war era was a mixture of high and low points. Aston Martin had gone through some glorious moments in the 1920s and 1930s but at the end of the war the small company was financially weak, and in 1947 had been taken over by the wealthy tractor manufacturer David Brown. Fortunately, he was a motoring enthusiast and encouraged the design staff to build a series of high performance GT cars. The modern range of cars started with the DB2, announced in April 1950. This car was powered by a straight six, twin overhead cam-shaft engine designed by W. O. Bentley of pre-war Bentley fame, and intended for a Lagonda model. In DB2 form the engine, which had a bore and stroke of 78 mm × 90 mm and capacity of 2580cc gave 105 bhp, but a 'Vantage' version was available, giving 120 bhp.

Both the engine and car were developed over the years, first into the DB2–4, and then the DB Mk 3 and eventually the DB4 of 1959. This was a high water mark for Aston Martin because their DBR1/300 won the World Sports Car Championship for them.

The six-cylinder all-alloy engine had been steadily developed over the years and for the DB4 it had been stretched to 3670cc and now gave more than twice its original power output – 240 bhp at 5500 rpm. The car itself retained a strong box section chassis with independent front suspension by wishbones and coil springs and a light live axle, tightly located by trailing arms and a Watt linkage. Disc brakes were fitted all round and steering was by rack and pinion.

The bodywork of the four seater DB4 was a fastback coupé shape designed by Touring of Milan and built on their Superleggera (super-light) principle, in which aluminium panelling is shaped round a network of small-diameter steel tubing. This was an expensive and time-con-suming process and the resultant cars were not cheap at £3755. The DB4 was not a light car and it required a strong pair of arms to conduct it round twisting roads at high speed, but on a straight road it would reach 140 mph. The ponderous gearbox needed treating with respect if the synchromesh was to remain intact and the DB4 was intolerant of poor maintenance, but it was a magnificent car to drive in anger.

A much more powerful variant was introduced in late 1959. This was the DB4GT, which had the engine tuned to give 302 bhp at 6000 rpm and also featured a number of other modifications such as a limited slip differential, a 30-gallon fuel tank and modified bodywork with a front-hinged bonnet and faired in headlamps. Although this car could be driven on the road it was largely intended for GT racing and it provided some memorable races against the 250GT Ferraris.

The standard DB4 was being constantly modified in little ways and in 1961 a convertible version appeared, this two-door four-seater being a very pretty car.

The engine power on the standard DB4 had remained at 240 bhp for some time, but in 1962 a Vantage version was announced, with power increased to 260 bhp at 5750 rpm. There were also several cosmetic modifications. A chunkily aggressive Zagato bodied version of the DB4GT also became available and this was also successful in racing, although only 25 were built.

The final model of the DB4 range was the Vantage GT, which had the trim of the Vantage model but the full 302 bhp GT engine. This full four-seater was as near a genuine 150 mph car as had been made in Britain at that time, although the E-type Jaguar ran close to it. Not many were made, however, and the DB5 replaced the DB4 in late 1963.

For many Aston Martin enthusiasts the DB4 was the best of the post-war cars. Previous cars were lacking in power while the later DB5 and 6 models put on weight and were more like fast tourers than high speed thoroughbreds.

THE 1960S —
'YOU'VE NEVER HAD IT SO GOOD'

Prosperity was rife by 1960 and although the people of many industrial countries grumbled, it was generally true that they had 'never had it so good'. Unemployment was low, the demand for consumer goods was high and the demand for new cars was insatiable.

The mood was nowhere better reflected than at the Jaguar factory in Coventry where the same team that had startled the motoring world in 1948 did it again in March 1961 when they announced the Jaguar E-type, or XK-E as it was known in the USA. The new model was as sensational as its predecessor because it brought very high performance within the reach of those with only just above average incomes.

The E-type had been developed from the successful D-type sports/racing car with its monocoque chassis. The E-type had a steel monocoque hull with deep side boxes, all welded up from steel pressings. At the front of the monocoque a square section steel frame was bolted on to take the front suspension and engine, while at the rear the suspension bolted into the monocoque chassis on its own subframe. Front suspension was by beautifully slim double wishbones in conjunction with torsion bars and telescopic dampers, while the rear suspension was by tubular lower links and double coil spring/damper units on each side, with the drive shafts acting as upper locating memberts. Disc brakes were fitted on all four wheels, the rear pair being mounted inboard adjacent to the differential.

All this was clothed in a sleek, low, curvaceous body of stunning beauty, which had been penned by Malcolm Sayer the man who designed the shape of the D-type. The family resemblance was obvious, but the E-type was even better.

Under the forward-hinging bonnet was the same twin-overhead camshaft six that had powered that very first XK120, except that it now displaced 3.8 litres, sported triple SU carburettors and gave 265 bhp at 5500 rpm.

The E-type Jaguar marked the last in the line of XK sports cars, which had started in 1948 with the 120. Introduced in 1961 with a 3.8-litre version of the famous twin-cam six, the beautiful car stunned the public, and it was not until 1974 by which time it had gained a 5.3-litre V12, that it finally died.

The E-type weighed in at around 22 cwt and it could accelerate from a standstill to 100 mph in 16 seconds and had a top speed in excess of 140 mph. Early magazine road tests showed a top speed of 150 mph, but Jaguar had fitted the test cars with racing tyres, which with their greater diameter gave a higher top speed, and of course the cars were very well prepared.

I ran an E-type coupé for a couple of years and could never make mine reach 150 mph, but even in the relatively traffic-free conditions of the early 1960s top speed was not vital. What was sensational about the E-type was that it would cruise happily for hour after hour at 130 mph, and then still have something left to *accelerate*! At 130 mph in the coupé wind noise was minimal and it felt like 70 mph in almost any other car.

However, E-type ownership was not altogether a bed of roses. It needed careful maintenance to keep it in good condition and little things went wrong with minor electrical components for no reason other than that they were built down to a price. The chassis also had 14 grease points, so it was not wise to trust the car to a dealer because if they were not greased the suspension soon became a mess.

The early E-type Jaguars were fitted with the same Moss gearbox as had been fitted to earlier Jaguars and although it was strong it was rough, having an unsynchronised first gear which sounded like an air raid siren. On a visit to Jaguar I asked an engineer about this and he said that they tested all gearboxes when they arrived from Moss and rejected a large proportion of them because of noise level. They placed a chalk mark on them and returned them to Moss, who promptly erased the chalk mark and sent them back to Jaguar!

Jaguar overcame this problem by designing their own gearbox, with baulk-ring synchromesh on all four gears. This appeared in 1964 along with a new 4.2-litre version of the old engine, which was claimed to give the same power output as the 3.8, but it would not rev in the same way

The AC Cobra series culminated in this, the 7-litre V8-engined 427. Unfortunately, this was fairly short-lived, as American regulations became too strict for it.

The result of the Maserati-Citroën alliance, the SM was powered by a 2.7-litre, 4 ohc V6 engine, developing 170 bhp, coupled to a front-wheel drive.

and the car was undoubtedly slower. The sweeter gearbox did make up for the loss of performance, though, and in any case it was still faster than most other vehicles on the road.

Of the two models available right from the start, the open two-seater was perhaps the most exhilarating to drive, but it had very little luggage space. The coupé had a very useful load space in the tail, which was reached through a sideways opening door, operated by a catch near the drivers seat.

Very conscious of the family man's market Jaguar introduced the E-type 2+2 coupé in 1966. This had a 9-in longer wheelbase and a pair of small rear seats. Unfortunately, this necessitated a higher roof line and a more upright windscreen, the resultant shape looking very bulbous and unattractive. Automatic transmission became available and the sports car image was all but lost.

American safety and exhaust pollution legislation began to affect cars exported to the USA, none more so than the E-type, and its beautiful shape was gradually nibbled away as first the front end was modified to fit headlamps that complied with US regulations, then the tail was chopped off to fit larger tail lamps. Exhaust emission modifications reduced the power output considerably on cars destined for the American market and sales began to decline inexorably and it seemed that as the 1960s ran out, the high performance or sporting machine was destined to be killed off in the interests of safety.

If the sports car had to die it was certainly going to go out with a bang, and a remarkable combination between a go-getting American and a staid British company saw to that. The American was Carroll Shelby and the British firm was AC, who had been doing well with their Ace-Bristol and Ace-Zephyr models.

In 1961 Shelby had recently retired from a career as a top class racing driver, in the course of which he had won the 1959 Le Mans 24 Hour race in an Aston Martin as well as numerous other races. Shelby wanted to build an all-

American sports car but could not get any backing, so he decided to look for a foreign chassis into which he could fit an American engine. After much deliberation he settled on the AC Ace and chose the 4.2-litre (260 cu in) Ford V8 as his power unit. The directors of AC agreed to fit an engine into a chassis and by late 1962 the completed car was despatched to the USA for testing. So successful were these tests that few modificaions were required and with backing from Ford, who were going back into racing in a big way, production got under way at the Thames Ditton factory. In England the car was known as the AC Cobra but in the States it was the Shelby American Cobra.

Although the power output had shot up to around 250 bhp from the modest 120 bhp of the Bristol and Ford Zephyr engines, the chassis was still very much as before and it seemed well able to handle the power. Shelby embarked on a competitions programme and soon the Cobra was doing well in all grades of sports and GT racing, from local club races up to international sports car races.

But the suspension, still with its transverse leaf springs, was quite primitive by racing standards and although it did well on smooth tracks it was handicapped on the bumpier roads of international events such as the Targa Florio, Nürburgring and Spa-Francorchamps and in 1964 a completely revised chassis with double wishbones and coil springs at both ends of the car was announced. The car had already lost its worm and peg steering system in favour of a rack and pinion layout, and the bigger 4.7-litre (289 cu in) V8 Ford engine giving 270 bhp had been standardised on the road cars.

So great was the demand for the Cobra that gradually all other AC models were abandoned, simply to allow space in the works for the ever increasing Cobra production.

In 1965 the already powerful Cobra was given yet another injection by dropping in the 7-litre (427 cu in) Ford V8 engine. This gave a power output of 425 bhp and endowed the Cobra with a top speed approaching 150 mph and acceleration figures which would not have disgraced a dragster a year or two before. A coupé model known as the Daytona was introduced, but this was retained for racing on high speed circuits where aerodynamic shape was important and very few were converted to road trim.

Unfortunately, the safety laws began to threaten the Cobra, as the flimsy aluminium body would not withstand the compulsory crash tests necessary to allow the car to be sold in America without substantial modifications. So, regretfully, production was stopped in 1968 after about 1100 cars had been built. A high proportion survive – indeed some enthusiasts joke that there are more on the road now than were ever made by AC, because high prices have encouraged one or two people to build cars up from spare parts.

AC continued the car in small scale production but fitted with a more luxurious body designed by Frua of Italy and renamed the AC 428.

One of the biggest surprises of the 1960s was provided by Daimler. This staidest of all British manufacturers, who usually built vast limousines for heads of state and other large saloon cars, suddenly announced their entry into the sports car market with a glass-fibre-bodied car called the SP250. The car was in fact announced in prototype form in 1959 at the New York Show but production did not begin until late that year.

The car featured a box type ladder chassis, strongly cross braced, with front suspension by double wishbones and coil springs, while at the rear the live axle was mounted on semi-elliptic leaf springs in conjunction with lever arm dampers. The chassis was underslung beneath the axle to give a low overall height. Steering was by cam and peg with only 2.6 turns lock to lock and braking was by Girling discs on all four wheels.

Power came from a very pleasant little V8 engine which used a cast iron block and alloy cylinder heads. The crankshaft ran in five main bearings and the overhead valves were operated by a central camshaft. With a compression ratio of 8.2:1 and twin SU carburettors the engine gave 140 bhp at 5800 rpm. This engine was mated to a four-speed all-synchromesh gearbox with the option of overdrive, or a fully automatic gearbox was available.

The bodywork, built of laid-up glass fibre mat at Daimler's Coventry works was undoubtedly ugly, having contrasting lines all over the body. By attempting to reach a halfway house between traditional sports car lines and the all-enveloping

shape that was already available on other cars, the Daimler fell between both camps. It was designed as a 2 + 2, although the rear pair needed to be quite small.

It was quite a good performer as it would reach a top speed of 124 mph and accelerate from 0 to 50 mph in 6.0 seconds. The effectiveness of its glass fibre body was demonstrated here, as at just under 19 cwt it was 3 cwt lighter than the Austin-Healey 3000. Unfortunately, the Healey cost £200 less than the Daimler, and this, combined with the Daimler's strange appearance, kept sales down.

Daimler recognised the faults of the SP250 and in April 1961 they introduced the SP250B with a much strengthened glass fibre body and a number of other small improvements. But the damage had been done and sales never reached an economic level. In any case Daimler had been taken over by Jaguar in 1960 and Jaguar felt that the E-type was quite sufficient for the new company. So in 1964 the SP250 was allowed to die, although Daimler engineers had been working on a very pretty body that might well have resuscitated the car.

Over in America Studebaker were struggling to stay alive in the early 1960s against the might of Ford, GM and Chrysler, and like so many small companies they produced some attractive looking cars to try to woo people away from the Big Three. Unfortunately, they had little money to spend on advanced engineering so used styling to do the job for them. Their aeroplane style propeller-spinner in the centre of the grille was a hallmark for several years and the Starliner, designed by Virgil Exner and Raymond Loewy was another landmark.

Despite this, Studebaker had to merge with Packard in 1954, and in 1956 the Starliner was revised to become the Hawk, while a supercharged version of the Packard V8 was fitted into the same car and named the Golden Hawk.

Although temporary relief came with the compact Lark which sold well the company was

The Daimler SP250 was either loved or hated; its style was certainly unusual. The glassfibre body created some problems, but the B version of 1961 was much improved. This car was built in 1960.

still in financial trouble and they decided to go into the sporting market, first with the GT Hawk of 1962 and then with the Avanti which went into production in 1963.

The Avanti was almost revolutionary by American standards for at that time only the Chevrolet Corvette could be considered at all sporting in concept. Naturally, Studebaker could not afford to design a completely new chassis so it was based on the 9 ft 1 in wheelbase chassis of the Lark compact car, but the box type ladder chassis was well cross-braced. Front suspension was by wishbones and coil springs with an anti-roll bar, while at the rear the live axle was mounted on semi-elliptic leaf springs and located by radius rods. Steering was by cam and peg while brakes were disc at the front and drum at the rear.

The standard model was fitted with a V8 engine of 4725cc (289 cu in) capacity which gave 210 bhp (SAE) at 4500 rpm on a compression ratio of 8.5:1 using a single Carter carburettor. A higher performance version of this engine gave 235 bhp by using a 10.25:1 compression ratio and a four barrel carburettor, whilst a high per-

The Studebaker Hawk GT of 1964. This marked the company's entry into the sporting market, having a 4.7-litre supercharged engine.

formance version with a capacity of 4.9 litres (304 cu in) gave 280 bhp at 4800 rpm using a Paxton supercharger.

A three speed gearbox was standard, but a four-speed was an option, as was a three-speed automatic and power steering. The only really unusual feature of the car by European sports car standards was the bodywork, a shovel-nosed 2 + 2 coupé with small round headlamps set into the nose, a style followed many years later by firms like Toyota and Vauxhall. The bodywork was made from glass-fibre-reinforced plastics and poor initial quality restricted sales in the early months. However, the car attracted a devoted band of followers in the States, mainly because of the high performance obtainable from the supercharged version, although few owners ever managed to see the 149 mph claimed for the blown model. It was quite popular in production

drag racing for a spell, but its modest chassis design gave it little chance of shining as a true sports car.

It could not hope to save Studebaker and in late 1963 the beginning of the end came when car production moved to Hamilton in Canada, and in 1966 the car-making side closed down altogether.

The Avanti survived for a while, as a dealer from Studebaker's old home at South Bend, Indiana took over production, simply naming the car Avanti II. Since 1964 all Studebakers had been powered by Chevrolet engines as it was not economic to continue production of Studebaker engines.

At the end of the 1950s the Austin-Healey 100–6 was evolved into the 3000. Bodily the car was very similar to the 100/6 with only the usual radiator grille and badging changes made to denote the differences. The model name 3000 was used because the engine capacity had increased from 2639cc to 2912cc. It was essentially the same BMC 'C' series engine as before but with twin SU carburettors and using a compression ratio of 9.03:1 it produced 124 bhp

The Avanti, like the Corvette was made of glassfibre; it was a popular machine, but Studebaker was already in some difficulties when it was announced in 1963, and the company closed down for good in 1966. This is the Studebaker Avanti II of 1967, manufactured by a one-time dealer.

at 4600 rpm. With a price of just under £1200 and top speed of 120 mph the 3000 was a popular buy, especially as the two small rear seats could be used for children, so that the family man was not precluded from buying a Healey.

In 1961 the power of the engine was increased to 130 bhp at 4750 rpm, which raised the top speed to around 124 mph, yet still allowed the car to give 20 mpg. The factory competitions department extracted even more power from the engine for rallying and over 200 bhp was quite common. This enabled some of its top rally drivers to win major international events such as the Liège-Rome-Liège twice and the Alpine Rally no less than three times, while it established the careers of drivers like Pat Moss who not only won the *Coupe des Dames* in many rallies but seriously embarrassed her male rivals on many occasions with her speed.

The 3000 was not the most sophisticated of sports cars and the term most often used to describe it was 'rugged'. The steering was not light, the gearbox needed care, the handling was not outstanding and the ride was firm to say the least, but anyone who drove one hard over a twisting route felt a great deal of satisfaction at having pushed this cumbersome sports car to its limit. Despite the ravages of 'British Racing Rust' as one disgruntled owner put it, the 3000 is still a much sought after car at ever increasing prices.

The two-seater 3000 had been dropped in 1962, leaving the 2 + 2 as the only model and this continued right to the end of production. Power output was raised again in 1964 with the introduction of the Mk III model. With bigger carburettors and internal engine modifications power was raised to 150 bhp at 5250 rpm. Acceleration did not improve dramatically as the gearing had been raised to give more relaxed driving.

As for so many other small volume production cars the American safety and pollution regulations spelled the end for the big Healey because although the sales to the States were still healthy the cost of modifying the car to meet the new regulations was too high and in 1968 the last 3000 was built.

Donald Healey, the man who dreamed up the Healey 100 idea back in 1952, did it again later on in the 1950s with the Austin-Healey Sprite, a miniscule sports car based on the mechanical components of the little Austin A35 saloon. He took the four-cylinder 948cc 'A' series engine, gave it twin SU carburettors and pepped up performance to 42.5 bhp at 5000 rpm and fitted it into an open two-seater with a monocoque chassis of great simplicity. There was no external boot and the forward end of the chassis was simply a punt into which the engine was dropped. The bonnet was practically the whole front of the car and it hinged at the rear to give excellent access. Front suspension was independent by wishbones and coil springs while the live axle was mounted on $\frac{1}{4}$-elliptic leaf springs and located by trailing arms. Drum brakes were fitted on all four

wheels and rack and pinion steering was standard.

With a dry weight of little more than 12 cwt the Sprite was the greatest possible fun to drive. It would just about scrape over 80 mph if the driver held on long enough (the official top speed was 81 mph) but whereas faster cars had to slow down for bends the experienced Sprite driver just kept his foot right up amongst the carburettors and scuttled round bends as if they were not there.

The Sprite bred an army of devoted fans, who referred to the strange bulging headlamps as 'frog eyes' and the Sprite soon became known as the 'Frog Eye Sprite' or 'Bug Eye Sprite'. It was amusing to watch a driver new to the car set off down the road because the steering was light and high geared and all new drivers proceeded in a series of swerves until they learned to steer with their fingertips. The odd gear ratios with far too low second and third gear ratios puzzled many drivers, but you simply revved like mad in third to make up for the jump into top.

BMC took a strange decision when they replaced the Mk I Sprite in May 1961, after only $2\frac{1}{2}$ years in production. The Mk II Sprite was an ugly slab sided, all-enveloping bodied car with all the creature comforts that the Mk I did not have and owners did not want. To add insult to injury BMC made a virtually identical version and had the effrontery to call it the MG Midget. Mk I Sprite owners still race them and care for them lovingly.

In France the great days of sports and luxury car production were long gone in the early 1960s. Names like Hispano-Suiza, Delage, Delahaye, Talbot, Bugatti and Hotchkiss had disappeared, killed off by the French car tax rating which inflicted punitive rates on cars over 2.8 litres. Only one manufacturer built road cars with engines over 2.8 litres in any quantity, and that was Facel Vega. The car was built not by a car manufacturer but by Facel Metallon, a toolmaking company which supplied much of the French motor industry. They also built bodies for several smaller companies, and when these contracts began to dry up, owner Jean Daninos decided to go into car manufacturing himself.

Instead of trying to keep under 2.8 litres he went the whole hog and designed the ultimate luxury car powered by the powerful $4\frac{1}{2}$-litre

Chrysler hemi-head V8. Daninos reasoned that anyone able to purchase his expensive cars would not be unduly worried by an annual car tax of £100.

The first car, simply called the Facel Vega was announced in 1954 and excited a great deal of interest among journalists and potential owners alike. The bodywork was slightly bulbous but undeniably attractive and the front end carried the distinctive radiator grille which was to remain with the car in various modified forms until the end.

The car developed into the HK 500 in 1960, by which time the car had the 6.2-litre (384 cu in) Chrysler engine which gave 360 bhp, endowing the car with a top speed of 140 mph and shattering acceleration for a big ($1\frac{3}{4}$ tons) car.

The Mk I, or Frog Eye, Sprite of 1958 was considered by the majority of enthusiasts to be the only Sprite worth looking at. Later ones were 'softer' and somehow less sporty. This is one of the last of the breed.

In 1962 the HK 500 developed into the Facel II, a much leaner, more attractive car. It was still a big two-door four-seater but weight had come down slightly, yet power had gone up as the Chrysler engine now gave 390 bhp (SAE) at 4800 rpm. The driver had the choice of a four-speed manual gearbox or the Chrysler Torqueflite three-speed automatic. With the former it was claimed that a top speed of 149 mph was possible along with a standing start $\frac{1}{4}$-mile time of 16.3 seconds.

The Facel Vega was one of the few French cars of the 1950s to ignore the punitive car tax on vehicles over 2.8-litres. Its maker reckoned that if people could afford the car then the road tax would not worry them. This is the HK500.

The interior of the car was sumptuously trimmed and the facia, trimmed in walnut, had so many switches and gauges that it was like the 'controls of a bomber' as one critic put it. Unfortunately, the price had risen to astronomic heights, and buyers could choose from other exotica such as Ferrari, Maserati, Bentley, Aston Martin etc. at about the same or even lower prices. The company had also taken the disastrous step of building its own sports car complete with their own twin cam engine. Although the new car, the Facellia, was pretty and sold well initially in both coupé and open form, its engine was very unreliable and owners soon suffered major defects with pistons, as the cooling system was incorrectly designed.

Although this problem was eventaully overcome public confidence was lost and an attempt to sell the car with the Volvo P1800 engine met with little success and the company also tried the Austin-Healey 3000 engine, reduced to 2.8 litres to beat the tax limit. This was no more successful and in 1964 the company was finally wound up.

The HK 500 and Facel II remain as two of the great White Elephants of all time and those that remain are eagerly sought after by enthusiasts prepared to pay very high prices.

In Italy, the long established firm of Lancia had survived precariously into the 1960s. The son of the company's founder, Gianni Lancia, had undertaken ambitious expansion plans and also developed a Grand Prix car, the Lancia D50, which showed great promise. Unfortunately, income from the sale of the firm's excellent range of cars was insufficient to meet outgoings and the Formula 1 cars were handed over to Ferrari, while expansion plans were abandoned. Despite the problems the company marketed a wide range of models at the start of the 1960s, including the Appia, Flavia and Flaminia, all technically advanced cars using widely differing mechanical components – a V4 engine in the Appia, a horizontally-opposed four in the Flavia and a V6 in the Flaminia. Consequently, they were expensive to build.

In 1964 Lancia replaced the Appia with the Fulvia saloon. Although its engine was a V4 it was a virtually all new engine with a different bore and stroke and with the cylinders canted over at an angle to obtain a low bonnet height.

This 1091cc engine gave 60 bhp at 5800 rpm, giving the chunky Fulvia saloon a top speed of 85 mph. Unlike its predecessor the Fulvia was a front-wheel-drive car, with a four-speed gearbox, while suspension on this unitary construction car was by wishbones and a transverse leaf spring at the front and a dead beam axle on semi-elliptic leaf springs at the rear. Worm and roller steering was used and brakes were a mixture of front discs and rear drums.

The saloon had no great impact but the pretty little coupé which followed in 1964 gained favour with sporting enthusiasts, and for them the engine capacity was increased to 1216cc and power output to 80 bhp at 6000 rpm. This gave a top speed of 105 mph, although acceleration was quite modest. The factory re-entered motor sport via rallying, and a roadgoing version of the rally coupé, called the HF, was marketed. This had a slight power increase, to 88 bhp, which put top speed up to 108 mph with a still modest acceleration rate.

Perhaps the most attractive of the Fulvia variants was the Sport. This was based entirely on the coupé chassis but was graced with an attractive coupé two-seater body designed by Zagato. This sleek fastback shape was very popular on the Continent and the hatchback rear door which was to become almost compulsory on family saloons of the 1970s, was raised by an electric motor.

The engine capacity increased steadily over the years. By 1970 it had grown to 1298cc and the power output of the Sport engine had increased to 103 bhp at 6000 rpm, pushing top speed to 112 mph. Finally the rally-developed engine increased in size to 1584cc and power went up to 114 bhp at 6000 rpm. By now a five-speed gearbox was standardised and top speed was a very respectable 115 mph, while a 0 to 50 mph time of 6.5 seconds was possible.

Although the Sport model never made a name for itself in competition its attractive good looks and combination of performance, handling and economy make it a collector's item.

By 1964 Porsche in Germany had established a world-wide reputation with their little 356 sports cars, but despite much development it was obvious that the flat four engine derived from the VW Beetle was nearing the end of its life. Porsche

had the perfect answer, for they added two cylinders and fitted the new flat-six engine into a completely new car. Initially named the 901, Porsche had to change the name to 911, because Peugeot had registered the title to all three figure numbers with a 0 in the middle. Despite various resemblances to the old 356 the 911 was an entirely new car and it taxed the little Porsche factory to the limit. In order to build sufficient bodies they took over the neighbouring Reutter coachworks.

The 911 featured an integral body/chassis unit, with front suspension by McPherson struts in conjunction with lower wishbones and longitudinal torsion bars while at the rear trailing arms and transverse torsion bars were used. Thus Porsche abandoned the swing axle which had aroused so much criticism on the 356. Steering was by rack and pinion and disc brakes were fitted on all four wheels.

The bodywork of the 911 was designed by Ferdinand Porsche's grandson, also called Ferdinand, and was essentially a lowered lengthened

Lancia's Fulvia had a long and distinguished career. This is the 1300cc version of the sporty Zagato coupé, built in 1971

356. Although the wheelbase was only increased by 4 in over that of the 356 to 7 ft $2\frac{3}{4}$ in, Porsche managed to squeeze in behind the two bucket seats a small bench seat which could take two children. Alternatively, the backrest could be folded down to provide a very useful luggage platform to supplement the rather meagre under bonnet space.

The six-cylinder engine was, in fact, very different from the four cylinder unit. The crankcase was in light alloy and the heavily finned cylinder barrels were also in light alloy. Each bank of cylinders was given a single overhead camshaft, driven by chain from the seven bearing crankshaft. With a bore and stroke of 80 mm × 66 mm the engine had a capacity of 1991cc. The first engine gave a power output of 130 bhp at 6200 rpm and it was mated to a five speed gearbox. Porsche considered placing the engine ahead of the gearbox to make the car a true mid-engined car, but this would have detracted from cockpit space and it was finally decided to retain the engine behind the gearbox, as on the 356.

The 911 was an immediate hit because its combination of performance and handling were almost unmatched at its price. So good was its shape that its top speed was a comfortable 130 mph, and, with a dry weight of under a ton, it would cover the standing start $\frac{1}{4}$-mile in 16.4 seconds. It was intended to keep the 356C in production for some time, but demand for the 911 was so high that it was dropped early in 1965; but a new model, the 912, fitted with the four-cylinder 90 bhp engine from the 356, was put into production.

Development of the 911 proceeded very rapidly and late in 1966 the 911S was announced. This had the engine tuned to give 160 bhp at 6600 rpm plus other modifications such as an anti-roll bar at the rear as well as the front, ventilated disc brakes, magnesium wheels and simplified trim which saved nearly 1 cwt over the normal 911. This model was capable of 140 mph in standard form and proved very popular with both ordinary road drivers and rally drivers.

Many critics claimed that the heavy rearward weight bias of the 911 would result in dangerous handling, and Porsche did add some extra weight at the front of the car to balance the handling, but in the hands of a good driver the Porsche was probably faster than any other road car. That it was a pretty fast car was shown in 1968 when Vic Elford won the Monte Carlo Rally outright over ice and snowbound roads.

Porsche models came thick and fast. The Targa model with its removable roof panel was very popular with fresh air fiends for a spell, while a lower powered version with 'only' 110 bhp and the old four-speed gearbox satisfied those who could not afford the more powerful versions. The 911E, with Bosch fuel injection, gave 140 bhp and the S with similar equipment went up to 170 bhp. Over the years engine capacity increased first to 2195cc, then in 1972 to 2343cc, then came the 2687cc version and finally

In 1964 the production of the Porsche 356 model came to an end. Shown here is the 2-litre Carrera model.

Porsche's amazing 911 series was born in 1964 and is still going in 1981, albeit in modified form. This is a somewhat non-standard 911 Targa of 1973.

the 2994cc version, which is still in production and in turbocharged form gives 260 bhp, still from the same basic flat-six configuration.

Although the 928 front-engined model has taken over as the flagship of the Porsche range there are those who maintain that the 911 was the last of the real Porsches. There are not too many who will disagree with that sentiment.

While all this development had been going on Ferrari had not been quiet and in 1962 he brought out one of the most breathtakingly beautiful yet powerful cars ever seen. This was the 250GTO, which was designed as both a road and racing car and was developed from the normal 250GT. No one is really sure what the 'O' at the end of the model name stands for, but the general consensus of opinion is that it means 'Omol-

Ferrari's 250GTO, designed both for road use and for racing. It won a string of races and rallies in the 1960s.

ogato,' the Italian for the word homologation, a term used in motor racing for a car that has been accepted into a particular racing category, as it meets the regulations of that class. This car used the familiar V12 engine, but in near full racing trim with six downdraught Weber carburettors and a power output of 300 bhp at 7400 rpm. It was mated to a new five-speed all-synchromesh gearbox, and suspension was very similar to the 250GT Berlinetta. The beautiful bodywork was built at the Ferrari works in aluminium and the trim was kept to a minimum. With only 20 cwt to pull the V12 engine gave the GTO a top speed approaching 180 mph and it soon began to notch up victories. A GTO won both the 1962 and 1963 Tourist Trophy races and one finished second overall in the 1962 Sebring 12 Hour race. For racing, the GTO was developed into the 330LM with a 4-litre version of the V12 giving 400 bhp at 7500 rpm. This was not very successful and Ferrari realised at this point that for racing success he would have to build mid-engined sports and GT cars, so the GTO was the last of the really great Ferrari front-engined cars. Although Ferrari guaranteed to build at least 100 GTOs for homologation purposes far fewer than this were actually built and those that remain are among the world's most covetable cars.

Only a few miles away from Ferrari's Maranello factory, the Maserati factory in Modena was not in such a happy position at the start of the 1960s. They had been obliged to give up Grand Prix racing at the end of the $2\frac{1}{2}$-litre Formula and existed on selling sports/racing cars and a few road cars to customers.

Maserati's main road engine was a straight-six, all aluminium unit with twin overhead camshafts driven by chain from the seven main bearing crankshaft. Surprisingly, this was fitted with Lucas fuel injection when this was in fairly early stages of development and in this form the engine gave 235 bhp at 5500 rpm.

The engine was fitted to the 3500GT coupé and GT coupé S, the latter car developing into the 3500GTI Sebring coupé. The Vignale coupé was undoubtedly one of the most handsome road cars in 1964, and it still is today. Very neatly proportioned, the Sebring was a 2+2 coupé with rear seats suitable for small adults. Claimed top speed in the fifth gear of its German ZF gearbox was 146 mph, although it is doubtful if this was really possible on the quoted power output, especially as the car weighed close to $1\frac{1}{2}$ tons ready for the road. The Sebring used a tubular steel chassis, with front suspension by double wishbones, coil springs and an anti-roll bar, while the live rear axle was mounted on semi-elliptic leaf springs and located by trailing arms. Steering was by recirculating ball and Girling disc brakes were fitted on all four wheels.

The Sebring was developed into the Mistrale, which appeared in both coupé and open two-seater form. The bodies of these two cars were designed by Frua and they bore a fairly close resemblance to the body which AC used on their 428 model.

Maserati had been building cars using a de-tuned version of the V8 racing engine for some years, but although the 5000GT was a catalogued model it was only built to order and very few of these 340 bhp, 170 mph cars were built. Unfortunately, the bodywork supplied as standard on the 5000GT looked very much like the body of the cheaper 3500GT and few wealthy owners wanted it to be thought that they 'only' owned a 3500, even though that car cost a hefty £5200 in 1963.

Towards the end of 1963 Maserati introduced a series production car using the V8 engine. This was the *Quattroporte* (four-door) which was a full four/five seater saloon with a semi-integral construction body designed by Carrozzeria Touring. Suspension was very similar to that of the sports models, but the wheelbase at 9 ft was over a foot longer than the Mistrale and the overall length was nearly two feet longer. The V8 engine had been tamed somewhat to make it quiet enough and reliable for a 'family' saloon. Capacity had been reduced to 4136cc and power was reduced to 290 bhp at 5200 rpm using four downdraught Weber 38DCNL carburettors. This engine was mated to a five-speed gearbox and Maserati claimed a top speed of 143 mph from this heavy (3638 lb) car.

Unfortunately, the *Quattroporte* was far too stodgy-looking to attract traditional Maserati and Ferrari customers and in any case it cost as much as a Rolls-Royce Silver Shadow, which gave far more comfort and prestige.

In an effort to win back lost sales Maserati came up with a beautiful two-seater coupé, the Ghibli, named after an African wind. Mechanically the car was similar to the *Quattroporte* but the V8 engine was increased in size to 4719cc, with a bore and stroke of 94 × 85cc and the power output was increased to 340 bhp at 5000 rpm using four Weber 38DCNL5 carburettors with an 8.8:1 compression ratio. Maserati claimed a top speed of 174 mph for the Ghibli but few independent testers got near this speed. However, the forte of the Ghibli was not its speed or handling but its staggering good looks. The bodywork curved gently right from the nose, with its quad headlamps hidden behind flaps, to the elegant fastback tail.

With a suspension layout that dated back to the 3500GT the Ghibli did not handle or steer very well and the more unkind road testers likened its behaviour to that of a fairly well-behaved truck. Certainly I found it quite a handful to try to drive fast on more sinuous roads, but this did not matter too much to buyers because it was a car in which to be seen. If you wanted to go fast in the mid-1960s you bought a Ferrari, Lamborghini, Jaguar or Porsche, leaving Maserati's and the like for the boulevard posers.

The Ghibli gave Maserati some respite from their ever-present financial problems but the arrival of the American safety and emission laws proved the final straw and in early 1968 a merger with Citroën was the only way out for the beleaguered Modenese company.

The early 1960s were exciting days for Ford of America because they had taken the decision to go into motor sport in a big way and also to build a smaller type of car with a sporting image. Their very clean-looking Falcon Sprints had done very well in the Monte Carlo rally because of their

excellent acceleration and good roadholding, and the eyes of European enthusiasts were being opened somewhat, because most Europeans felt that all American cars were suspended on marshmallow springs with about as much directional stability as a blancmange. They were soon to be proved wrong. I was privileged to drive one of the Monte Carlo Rally cars and I was staggered at the prodigous acceleration imparted by the 4.2-litre V8. The car had been geared down to give a top speed of little more than 110 mph, as acceleration was the main requirement on the Monte Carlo rally, and that car went like a scalded cat. The rally cars had disc brakes on the front wheels which had been given a pounding on the rally and I was forced into an embarrassing spin when I had to slam on the brakes to avoid a wandering tank on the tank-testing track where I was trying out the car. But I parted with that car very reluctantly, having found a new respect for American cars.

By coincidence, in 1964 I went to America to report the Indianapolis 500 mile race, just a week or so after Ford had announced their new sporty compact, the Mustang. Ford loaned me one to drive from Detroit to Indianapolis and back and I experienced the tremendous surge of interest that

A Maserati 3500GT, fitted with Bertone rather than Vignale coachwork.

this car had created among the public. Everywhere I stopped, the car was surrounded by curious onlookers, all asking questions about it. The Mustang was the first of the so called 'pony' cars, the nickname given to the new breed of sporting compact cars that Ford had invented. The in-joke that was flung at all owners of Mustangs in the first few weeks of its life was, 'I see you got one of them new fangled horse-drawn vee hicles'. Soon, so many people had those 'horse drawn vee-hicles' that the joke died rapidly.

The Mustang was not particularly innovative technically, but to Americans, fed on an almost unrelieved diet of huge cars, the Mustang was something new. With a wheelbase of 9 ft and overall length of 15 ft 3½ in it was quite tiny compared with some American leviathans which could have wheelbases of nearly 11 ft and an overall length of 19 ft. It had an integral unit-construction chassis when most American cars still had ladder-type separate chassis, and front suspension was independent by wishbones, coil springs and telescopic dampers while the live rear axle was mounted on semi-elliptic leaf springs and telescopic dampers. The cheaper models had a straight-six 3277cc (200 cu in) engine giving 120 bhp at 4400 rpm, mated to a three speed gearbox, but most buyers opted for the more exotic specifications. The most popular engine was the 4.7-litre (289 cu in) V8 giving power outputs ranging from 220 to 270 bhp (SAE), but there was also a 6.3-litre (390 cu in) V8 giving 320

bhp (SAE) at 4800 rpm. The optional four speed gearbox was also very popular but the Cruise-o-Matic three speed automatic was also available.

There was also a tremendous choice of extras, and buyers could tailor the car to their own specifications. Drum brakes were standard fittings but front disc brakes were optional as were various suspension modifications and extra instrument packages. The 'softies' could even specify air conditioning. The Mustang was available as a two-door hardtop, a convertible and a fastback coupé, all of which became immensely popular. The Fastback was very popular with racing enthusiasts because of its better aerodynamic shape, and even in standard form fitted with the 6.3-litre engine it was capable of 130 mph. This engine was somewhat heavier than the 4.7-litre V8 and most keen drivers opted for the latter as it still gave a top speed of 115 to 120 mph, yet the car handled much better because it was better balanced.

For a long while the Mustang swept all before it, giving Fords some of the best sales figures they had ever had. It did well in many races and rallies and even more powerful versions were built, notably the Shelby American GT350 version. This model, a Fastback coupé, was heavily modified by Carrol Shelby to give 306 genuine horsepower, not the anaemic horse-power generally quoted by American manufacturers. Another hot version was the Mach 1 which succeeded the Shelby 350GT and was also based on the Fastback.

But by the early 1970s the Mustang was no longer news and although it carried on for many years it no longer had any real importance in the American Ford range, and although the name continues today it is attached to an even smaller, rather unremarkable car.

Despite the steady swing towards smaller cars the majority of American drivers in the 1960s still loved their big cars, and the two American luxury makes, Lincoln and Cadillac, still sold by the hundred thousand rather than the few hundred that European luxury car makers could expect to sell in a year. The Lincoln company had been started by Henry Leland, who had previously been a precision tool maker. When he started Lincoln, named after President Lincoln, he insisted on the same quality in his cars and some

*By 1963 Ferrari were offering this 'Super Lusso'
version of the famous 250GT, with bodywork by
Pininfarina.*

very fine cars were produced in the 1920s. Unfortunately, Leland ran into financial difficulties and the only man who could bail out Lincoln was Henry Ford. Leland and Ford could not get on together and soon Ford had taken complete control of Lincoln, making it a division of the Ford Motor Company.

Despite the change of ownership the quality of Lincoln cars remained high and one of the highlights was the Lincoln Zephyr of 1936, a V12 engined car which sold extremely well. A sporting version of the Zephyr with much lower body lines was designed by stylist Eugene Gregoire and introduced in 1939. Called the Continental, simply because of its vaguely European styling, it used Zephyr parts, including the V12 engine and had a distinctive mounting for the spare wheel which was placed vertically at the rear of the boot. Although occasionally dropped, this Lincoln hallmark appears on a large number of the Continentals made ever since.

After World War II the Zephyr model was dropped but the Continental survived for a short while with the V12 engine but by 1948 it was ousted in favour of cheaper Lincolns using many Ford parts.

The Continental name was revived in 1956 on a two-door coupé with the rear mounted spare wheel. This was in fact little more than a standard 6-litre Ford model, but the interior was given the luxury treatment of leather seating, pile carpeting, extra instruments, and a radio as standard. Unfortunately its very high price tag of $9500 attracted few customers and the Mk II Continental, as it was called, sold only 3012 examples in two years, a sufficient guarantee of exclusivity in itself.

Slightly modified versions of the Mk II named the Mk III and IV, were built until 1960 but for 1961 a brand new Continental was announced. This car featured a long low body shape, the main model being a pillar-less four door saloon, with the front doors being forward hinged and the rear doors hinging at the rear, allowing very easy access. A similar looking convertible model was very popular. Technically, the cars were similar to equivalent Ford models, but the cars were inspected carefully and given a 10-mile road test before delivery.

The standard engine of the Continental was the 7030cc (430 cu in) V8 which gave 320 bhp (SAE) at 4800 rpm and this was mated to the Turbo-Drive three speed automatic transmission. Top speed was a comfortable 114 mph Mechanically, the Continental was 'standard American' with an integral construction chassis, front suspension by wishbones, coil springs, telescopic dampers and an anit-roll bar, while the live rear axle was mounted on semi-elliptic leaf springs and telescopic dampers. Braking was by servo assisted drums all round and steering was by recirculating ball.

With an overall length of over $17\frac{1}{2}$ ft and a dry weight of 46 cwt the Lincoln was not the sort of car to throw around bends but it gained prestige simply from its sheer size and grandeur. Over the years the styling changed subtly at first and engine size crept up to $7\frac{1}{2}$-litres, but by 1970 the classic convertible model had gone and only the saloon retained four doors. The slab sided look had been replaced by a kicked-up tail treatment and the horizontal grille had been replaced by a central grille which owed more to Rolls-Royce than anyone else. The headlamps also disappeared behind flaps. The external spare wheel lived on merely as a semi-circular indentation in the boot lid.

The Continental received the ultimate accolade in 1968 of being chosen as the Presidential limousine, although after the necessary bulletproofing of bodywork and glass, plus extensive communications equipment had been installed it cost an astonishing half a million dollars.

Although the Lincoln gained a fine name in America as a luxury car only Cadillac could really be equated with Rolls-Royce in America. Before the war Cadillac had produced many fine cars, none more so than the legendary V16, introduced in 1930. Some splendid bodies were built on the Cadillac V16 and later V12 chassis by Fleetwood, their best known bodybuilder. After the war Cadillac moved to V8 engines and bodied their cars with some of the ugliest creations yet seen. They 'invented' the tail fin, after copying it from an aircraft, and also fitted the cars with huge chrome plated radiator grilles and massive chrome bumpers of indescribable bad taste.

This was sad, because underneath the horrific bodywork of the 1949 model was the first of the modern overhead valve V8s which still grace most American cars today. This 5420cc (331 cu in) engine gave 160 bhp, giving the Cadillac a top speed of over 100 mph and it soon attracted the attention of sports car specialists, who began dropping Cadillac engines into their specials. One of the most successful was of course the Allard, which won many a race with Cadillac power under the bonnet, while Briggs Cunningham even took a Cadillac car to race at Le Mans – and it was not disgraced.

Fortunately, the tail fin and porthole era passed, and by the early 1960s Cadillac's began to look clean and impressive, even though a vestigial tail fin hung on until 1965. By 1964 the V8 had shot up to 6.4-litres (390 cu in) and 325 bhp (SAE) while you would need a garage at least 19 ft

long just to squeeze in a Cadillac. The Fleetwood name was retained and this was reserved for the larger more stately limousines beloved by heads of state, ambassadors and funeral parlours.

Some of the cleanest looking Cadillacs were the 1967 range, with a smooth body style and styling reminiscent of the rival Lincoln. Engines were now up to 7-litres (429 cu in) and 340 bhp (SAE) so that most models would top 120 mph. One of the most handsome models was the Fleetwood Eldorado, a two-door hardtop of very pleasant dimensions. Technically, it was almost revolutionary by American standards for it featured front wheel drive. This was not an original Cadillac design but had been borrowed from their GM stablemate Oldsmobile, who had been using it on the Toronado model for two years. Unfortunately, this innovation brought no real advantages for the traditional Cadillac buyer many of whom probably did not know the front

The 3-litre V12 of the 250GT Super Lusso, with its triple Weber carburettors.

wheels were the driven ones.

The American exhaust and safety laws began to catch up with Cadillac, while a new law stating that all manufacturers had to supply a range of cars averaging 27 mpg overall by the early 1980's forced Cadillac to cut down on their massive range and introduce a small car. This model, the Seville, with an overall length of 'only' 17 ft and a 'tiny' 5.7-litre V8 giving 180 bhp (SAE) was small by their standards and gave a fairly firm indication of the way the American industry was having to move, faced with a shortage of fuel.

Oldsmobile's Toronado was a design innovation of almost earth shattering proportions in the USA, because the only engineering advance considered necessary in the mid-1960s was to extract as much horse power as possible from the universal V8 engine. Not only was it a phenomenal advance but it gave a salutary lesson to European engineers who had stated quite categorically that front wheel drive would show no advantage when used in conjuction with engines of more than 2-litres. In fact they felt that excessive wheelspin and poor steering characteristics would make any front wheel drive car with a big engine quite terrifying to drive. The

The Ford Mustang began its life in 1964 and immediately attracted huge sales. This photograph depicts the 1967 Mustang range of 2 + 2, hardtop and convertible.

Oldsmobile engineers not only used an engine over 2-litres, they fitted a huge 6.9-litre (425 cu in) V8 giving a power output of 385 bhp (SAE) at 4800 rpm. This great engine drove the front wheels via a two-stage torque converter which drove via a chain and sprocket a three-speed automatic gearbox which was situated beside the block of the V8. From the gearbox the drive was taken forward by shaft to the hypoid bevel drive with planetary differential.

Mechanically, the Toronado was little different from other American cars, having a perimeter ladder type frame, front suspension by wishbones, torsion bars and an anti-roll bar while the dead beam rear axle was mounted on semi-elliptic leaf springs in conjunction with no less than four telescopic dampers. Braking was by power assisted 11-in drums on all wheels and steering by power assisted Saginaw recirculating ball steering.

All this was clothed in an attractive two door,

The name Continental represents a whole range of cars built over many years by Lincoln, Ford's quality marque. This is the 1963 style.

four seater coupé body with fastback tail, which
looked brutal yet attractive. Unfortunately, the
stylists took little advantage of the space savings
they could have made with the forward location
of the power unit and the rear seat was rather
cramped.

The amazing feature of the Toronado was the
fuss-free way the front wheel drive worked. To
drive the car you simply plonked your throttle
foot down and away the car sped. It did not spin
its wheels unless very aggressive driving tech-
niques were used and it would corner quite
neutrally. If really high speed cornering was
attempted it *would* run wide, just like any other
front wheel drive car but if the throttle foot was
lifted it would pull back onto line again, just like
any other front wheel drive car. All this was
accompanied only by the rustle of the tyres on the
road, because the V8 was as quiet as a mouse.

Where the Toronado really scored over its
American rivals was in traction on a wet road.
Conventional rear wheel drive American cars are
practically uncontrollable in wet conditions. I
remember once sitting at a set of traffic lights in
the USA on a wet road behind a big American
car, the driver of which wanted to turn left. When
the lights turned green he accelerated away,
turned the steering wheel to the left and the tail of

*The Bertone-bodied Lamborghini Espada was
developed as a four-seat production family car, yet
it handled well and could reach 150 mph.*

the car spun right round until the driver came to a
stop facing me, looking round in a puzzled way,
wondering how he had got in that position! With
the Toronado the front wheels simply pull the car
round bends and the rear wheels cannot break
traction.

Sadly, few American drivers appreciated the
benefits of front wheel drive at the time, and in
truth for 80 per cent of the time on wide Freeways
it was of no benefit, but when traction was needed
the Toronado had it in plenty.

Oldsmobile persevered with the design into
the 1970s but it never took over in the way front
wheel drive has in Europe, and now more
Americans are driving front wheel drive
European cars than ever bought Toronado's.

It took mighty General Motors just two years
to catch up on Ford's early lead with their
Mustang 'pony' car. Their answer, announced in
1966, was the Chevrolet Camaro, a two door
sporting car available as either a coupé or
convertible. Just like the Mustang it was smaller
than the usual 'standard' size American car with a

wheelbase of 9 ft and overall length of 15 ft 4 in. The chassis was a mixed integral and ladder frame with front suspension by the ubiquitous double wishbones and coil springs and a rear axle on semi-elliptic leaf springs. Brakes were drum all round on standard models and steering was by recirculating ball. There was nothing particularly outstanding technically on the Camaro, but with a dry weight of around 27 cwt and a good looking body it sold like the proverbial hot cakes. As with the Mustang, the owner could more or less tune the car to suit himself. The choice of engines was wide, ranging from the basic 3769cc (230 cu in) 140 bhp straight-six up to a 5735cc (350 cu in) V8 giving 295 bhp (SAE) at 4800 rpm.

The choice of transmissions was equally wide, as drivers could order a three speed manual, a four speed manual or a two speed automatic gearbox. Power assisted steering, which lowered the steering ratio to three turns lock to lock, was optional, as were front disc brakes. Many suspensions were available for both road and racing versions and interior trim and paintwork were options.

Performance could be almost exactly what the buyer wanted, from a modest 98 mph from the six cylinder to a hefty 122 mph from the most powerful V8. This almost exactly paralleled Ford's marketing strategy with the Mustang and although General Motors were officially out of racing they provided backing for the Roger Penske team to enter TransAm saloon car racing. With Mark Donohue at the wheel the team won two TransAm series against heavy opposition from Ford and American Motors. This model, the Z28 was a heavily modified car with a highly tuned V8 of 5-litres, which was the maximum engine capacity for the TransAm series. Many suspension options were available and the Camaro was soon appearing in races all over the world. Some of the earlier Z28s are still winning races today.

The Camaro continued in essentially unchanged external form until 1970 when a completely new body shape was revealed. It had the same wheelbase and the mechanical layout was very similar to its predecessor but the body shape was subtly altered, retaining the kicked-up 'Coke bottle' shape of the rear end but modernising the shape of the rest of the body, with a rectangular grille replacing the more horizontal version of the first model.

Unfortunately, American safety laws killed off the convertible model, but the Z28 returned and it was joined by another sporting variant the SS, which looked very sporty with its half-bumpers at the front and hefty tail spoiler. Sadly, the pollution laws stifled development of the Camaro and the more powerful engine options have gradually been dropped. For the stringent smog laws of California there is even a pitiful version which gives 90 bhp from its six cylinder 4097cc (250 cu in) engine, exactly 50 bhp *less* than the smaller six gave in 1966!

It is little wonder that the most highly prized Camaro's are those made in the late 1960s, especially the Z28 with its macho appearance and staggering performance.

At Chrysler, executives did not intend to let rivals get away from them in the power race and it was left largely to their Dodge Division to uphold the prestige of the Chrysler Corporation. They did not go for a Mustang/Camaro challenger but opted to stay in the 'muscle' car league as the bigger cars were called. They used two cars to keep up their performance image, the Charger and the Challenger. The Charger was campaigned in the NASCAR stock car events so it had to have a big powerful engine. It was big at 7210cc (440 cu in) and it was powerful, with optional outputs of 375 or 390 bhp. There was a smaller yet even more powerful version available, the 6981cc (426 cu in) V8 which gave 425 bhp (SAE) at 5000 rpm. It also gave a massive 490 lb ft of torque at 4000 rpm, so it didn't matter much which gear a Charger or Challenger was in. In this form a Charger or Challenger coupé would comfortably exceed 130 mph, with acceleration to match.

The cars were fairly conventional American machines with integral chassis/body units, front suspension by wishbones and torsion bars and live rear axles on semi-elliptic leaf springs. Transmission was either a four speed manual or three speed automatic and drum brakes were standard, but front discs could be specified. A large list of performance options and axle ratios could also be specified. The Charger could be had only as a two-door hardtop but the Challenger came as a two door hardtop, two door convertible

and a four door special hardtop. The bodies of the Charger and Challenger were long, low, wide and handsome, with a wide, open front grille and the popular kicked up tail treatment. The 1970 models were really the end of Dodge 'muscle' cars and although the Charger and Challenger carried on they were mere shadows of their former powerful selves as the Chrysler Corporation bowed to the safety lobby.

In the mid 1960s American V8s still provided the basis for many a European hybrid. One of these was the ISO, a small firm building cars by hand near Milan. Their two main models were the Rivolta and the Grifo, the former being a four seater saloon while the latter was an attractive two seater coupé. Unusually for a small scale production car the Grifo was an integrally constructed car with the steel bodywork built up on and welded to the stout tubular steel side members. Suspension was independent by wishbones and coil springs while a de Dion axle, located by fore and aft and lateral links, and suspended on coil springs was fitted at the rear. Big servo assisted Dunlop disc brakes were fitted all round and steering was by Burman recirculating ball steering.

Power came from the Chevrolet 5359cc (324 cu in) V8 which gave a power output of 365 bhp at 6200 rpm. This engine was mated to the excellent Warner four speed all-synchromesh gearbox. Not unaturally, with a dry weight of around 27 cwt the Grifo was very quick and I still have vivid memories of driving a blood red example when it was introduced in 1966. The acceleration was staggering, as it could reach 100 mph in less than 17 seconds from a standstill and go on to a top speed of 160 mph, which was certainly the fastest I had ever travelled in a road car at that time. Although the Warner gearbox was far better than most European gearboxes because it was so strong and silent as well as having excellent synchromesh, it was hardly needed. When driving gently all that was needed was to move off in first gear and almost as soon as the car was rolling the gear lever could be popped into top gear.

The 1975 edition of Cadillac's Eldorado. Front-wheel drive, a feature of the Eldorado, was probably of no interest to the average buyer.

The car also had incredibly good roadholding because it simply went round bends; it needed no special technique or skill. The driver simply turned the steering wheel and round it went. The driver had no need to worry about understeer or oversteer because it didn't exist unless the driver did something extremely foolish.

The Grifo was one of the very fine cars of the 1960s which deserved much wider sales than it really achieved. Unfortunately, ISO did not have an exotic name like Ferrari and Maserati and the car was powered by a cheap American engine, so it didn't appeal to the type of people who could afford it. It was also very expensive, since one could buy three E-type Jaguars for the £6000 price tag of a Grifo.

A special version of the Grifo called the Bizzarini, built by Gioto Bizzarini, was made for a short while and intended mainly for competition. I drove one briefly and found it to be even faster than the Grifo, as I was timed on the M1 at 174 mph. I reported this to the owner who seemed unimpressed; he lifted the boot lid and showed me a massive set of American carburettors and manifolds which he reckoned would take

Oldsmobile's Toronado introduced front-wheel drive to the large car, amid suspicion from European engineers. This picture of a 1968 car shows it to be quite attractive compared with some of the opposition.

the car comfortably over 180 mph!

One of the most epoch making high performance cars of the 1960s was born out of one man's feeling that he had been slighted. The car is the Lamborghini and the man is Ferruccio Lamborghini. He made his fortune after the war making tractors out of any old parts he could find and gradually expanded the business until he was also making central heating and air conditioning systems. He soon got into a position where he could enjoy the good things of life and with his passion for cars he began to buy Ferraris from the Maranello factory which was situated not far from his tractor factory in Bologna. However, one day Lamborghini felt that he had been slighted by Enzo Ferrari while he was on a visit to the factory and walked out vowing to make a car that was better than any Ferrari. No doubt this

Chevrolet's answer to the Mustang was the Camaro. This is a fairly early 1967 example.

story is exaggerated, because Lamborghini had had ambitions to build cars for many years, but it no doubt spurred him into action.

The first Lamborghini caused a sensation at the 1963 Turin Motor Show because it was technically the equal of anything that Ferrari had yet produced. The 350GTV as it was called was powered by a V12 engine of 3463cc (211 cu in) with very over-square cylinder dimensions of 77 × 62 mm. With twin overhead camshafts per bank of cylinders, a sturdy seven bearing crankshaft, dry sump lubrication, six down-draught Weber 38IDL twin choke carburettors and a compression ratio of 9.5:1 it gave a very healthy 290 bhp at 6500 rpm.

The chassis of the 350GTV was a strong mixture of tubular steel ladder frame and box members, while suspension was all-independent by double wishbones and coil springs. Steering was by worm and roller and big servo assisted disc brakes were fitted to all four wheels.

The coupé was capable of speeds of around 150 mph and acceleration to match Ferrari production 250 models, but the bodywork by Super-leggera Touring was not particularly attractive

and Lamborghini soon had plans to build additional models to supplement and eventually replace the 350 and later 400GTV models.

Few people were prepared for the sensational new model that eventually appeared from the Bologna factory. Lamborghini's brilliant young designer Gian Paolo Dallara came up with a sensational new mid engined car, named the Miura, after a fierce breed of Spanish fighting bull (spelt Muira in Spanish). This car had a development of the original V12 engine, now increased to 3929cc (239 cu in) and giving 350 bhp at 7000 rpm. The engine was mounted transversely across the rear of the car driving to a five speed gearbox. The entirely new chassis had double wishbones and coil springs at both ends, disc brakes all round and rack and pinion steering.

The elegant coupé bodywork of the Miura was attractive yet functional and would not have disgraced a racing GT coupé. Naturally it was strictly a two-seater with barely any room for luggage, but if you had the £8500 to buy a Miura in 1966 then you could afford to send on your luggage in the Rolls.

Some drivers found the Miura claustrophobic, because there was little room in the cockpit, the seating position was low and rearwards visibility was negligible, due to the use of a slatted venetian blind type of rear window covering. But once on the move no red-blooded driver needed to worry about the rear view because nothing would overtake a determinedly driven Miura. The factory claimed a top speed of 300 kilometres an hour (186 mph) which was rather ambitious and although many people tried, it would really only do about 170 mph! To try to get over 180 mph Lamborghini introduced the Miura S model with the engine uprated to give 370 bhp at 7700 rpm, and they still claimed 186 mph for this version, but it wouldn't reach it either. Not that this really mattered because it would reach 150 mph ridiculously quickly and this is as much as anyone could really hope to cruise at even on the relatively uncrowded roads of the mid 1960s.

The forté of the Miura was its near racing car handling abilities and with its dry weight of just over a ton it was electrifyingly quick under all conditions. It was just as happy storming a mountain pass as flying along a motorway at terminal velocity.

Lamborghini never seemed to rest on their laurels for long, and not long after the Miura they brought out the Espada, a full four seater, but a very futuristic looking one. It was based on an experimental show car, the Marzal, which many observers felt was simply a quirky 'dream car', but they reckoned without Lamborghini, who turned the car into a thoroughly practical family man's Supercar. In the Espada the V12 engine was mounted at the front and tuned to virtually the same trim as in the Miura, so that the driver had 350 bhp on tap. The Espada had a very similar chassis to that of the other front engined Lamborghini's but it had a lengthened wheelbase of 8 ft 8.3 in and an overall length of 15 ft 6.5 in. It also turned the scales at nearly 3000 lb, so it was not lightweight, but it could still do 150 mph and handled extremely well for such a big car. Although it cost as much as a Miura it was quite popular by Supercar standards as the rear seats

meant that it could be used as a family car. Indeed it was the only car that Lamborghini built which was a regular production car – in other words, a car would go along the production line even before there was an order for it, whereas the other models were only started when an order came in for them.

In 1965 there were many people who were beginning to wonder if the Rolls-Royce was still the best in the world. True, the Silver Cloud III was imposing and impressive to look at but it was no quieter than a Cadillac or Lincoln, it was slower than dozens of other luxury limousines and its cornering ability could only be described as ponderous. Even Rolls-Royce had to move with the times and they did so with the Silver Shadow, an entirely new design which aroused both admiration and controversy. Gone was the graceful sweep of the front wings of the Silver Cloud, gone the delicate curve of the rear wings and gone the stately Palladian look of the massive Rolls-Royce radiator. In its place we had a modern slab sided saloon on an integral construction chassis, independent suspension on all four wheels for the first time and a cut down version of the famous radiator.

The critics had a field day. Most of the criticism was aimed at the body shape, because most of the critics felt that the anachronistic appearance of the older models was half the reason for the make's continuing popularity. Crusty colonels trumpeted that the Silver Shadow looked like nothing more than an overblown Vanden Plas Princess. And, to be honest, there was some truth in the criticism, but once the initial furore was over, sales of the Shadow began outstripping those of its predecessors, so much so that there always was a two year waiting list for a Silver Shadow.

The integral chassis/body unit was so designed that specialist coachwork could still be fitted and both H. J. Mulliner and James Young built special saloon bodywork almost from the start.

To ensure a silent ride the front and rear suspension is mounted on subframes, insulated from the main chassis and the front suspension is by wishbones and coil springs while the rear suspension is by semi-trailing arms and coil springs. A self levelling system was built in, powered by the car's high pressure hydraulic

system, but unlike the Citröen system which constantly levelled the car throughout a journey, over all types of road surface, the Rolls-Royce layout was simply fitted to cope with different numbers of passengers and luggage contents.

The Shadow was the first Rolls to have disc brakes fitted and the designers went to elaborate lengths with three braking circuits, to ensure that they were adequate for their task. Over the years Rolls-Royce engineers were often quizzed about their reluctance to use discs, but they would always reply that they would use them when their performance and quietness met Rolls-Royce standards. It would obviously never do if a Rolls-Royce brake actually squeaked!

The light-alloy 6.2-litre V8 engine was retained in almost unchanged form but the four speed automatic gearbox, which was retained for

The Charger was Dodge's 'muscle car' of the mid 1960s. It could be had with a 425 bhp engine, which made it very popular and very successful in competition. This one was made in 1967.

a while on the Shadow was replaced by a more modern three speed unit, again from General Motors of America.

Naturally, the car is trimmed with the finest wood and leather. The leather comes from Scandinavia where cows are not bitten by insects or snagged on barbed wire and the dashboard and door panels are veneered with Circassian walnut which is matched with almost clinical care. So great is Rolls-Royce's attention to detail that a piece of each walnut log is retained and marked with the chassis number of the car on which the

rest of the log has been used. Should the car be damaged in an accident or the walnut veneer be damaged, Rolls-Royce will then be able to supply an exactly matching piece of veneer. It almost goes without saying that the floor of the car and boot are carpeted with Wilton carpet.

Another factor that had to be taken into account when designing the Shadow was that the day of the chauffeur was beginning to decline so the car had to be designed for the owner-driver. Therefore, seating was given much more consideration as were factors such as leg room, instrumentation and car radio. Unfortunately, the day of the cocktail cabinet, vanity case and other apurtenances of gracious Rolls-Royce living were absent, although the specialist coachbuilders could still supply them to order.

The Shadow was no slouch when it was introduced, having a top speed of 120 mph and acceleration that was more than adequate, if hardly in the sports car class. Where the car did come in for criticism was in the softness of its suspension, which was fine for cruising over poorly surfaced roads but cornering produced a great deal of roll, even at quite modest speeds. It was felt not quite right to have the Duchess topple over as the car hustled round bends and before long a number of modifications were made to both the suspension and tyres to improve the situation. Although the car never became a high speed corner-eater later models can cover the ground astonishingly rapidly.

The same year that the Silver Shadow was announced the Rootes Group, based in Coventry, made a radical alteration to their pretty but unremarkable Sunbeam Alpine sports car. The normal power unit was the Rootes 1592cc engine but this was replaced by the very same Ford 4.2-litre V8 engine which had been the basis of the astonishing AC Cobra. Set well back in the chassis and mated to the four speed

Gordon-Keeble had a troubled career, with a certain amount of stopping and starting. Their luxury cars were of high quality and high performance, being eventually powered by a 5.4-litre Chrysler V8. Styled by Bertone they were originally built in steel, but all production cars were of glassfibre.

American Ford gearbox this engine gave a comfortable 141 bhp at 4400 rpm, compared with the 82 bhp of the 'normal' Alpine!

Naturally, the result was predictably electric. Top speed jumped from 102 mph to 120 and the 0 to 50 mph time came down from 9 to 7 seconds. Since the car named Tiger, sold at a relatively modest £1445 in open two seater form enthusiasts eagerly snapped up this hot performer. Although the car retained its wishbone and coil spring front suspension and rigid rear axle on leaf springs, they were naturally uprated to cope with the extra weight and power, while the recirculating ball steering of the smaller engined model was replaced by a rack and pinion layout and the brakes were beefed up.

The result was a very entertaining car which had its limitations. The ride was quite firm and on bumpy roads it could get quite exciting, while the rear wheels could be made to break traction with a hefty prod on the throttle in low gears. It was a tricky car to drive fast in the wet, but that was what made it such fun for owners.

The Rootes competition department built some very hot versions of the car for racing and rallying, which promised well for a return to international success. Sadly, the American Chrysler Group took control of the Rootes Group, and they were faced with the embarrassment of having one of their cars fitted with an American Ford engine. Initially, plans were made to fit the car with a Chrysler engine but none of the big Chrysler V8s were really suitable and in June 1967 after little more than 18 months in production the Tiger was discontinued. Since the chassis was rather prone to rusting not too many Tigers remain on the road, although fortunately many are in the drier climates of California where they are being well preserved.

Despite Chrysler's inability to squeeze one of their V8s into a car that they were making, their engines were still very popular with the British specialist manufacturers like Bristol and Jensen. The latter fitted a big hemi-head Chrysler V8 into one of the most advanced cars of its time, the Jensen FF, which was announced in 1966. The FF stood for Ferguson Formula, which was the four wheel drive system pioneered by the late Harry Ferguson and still being developed by the company he founded, now led by ex-racing

Lamborghini's splendid 350GT of 1965. The 350 was the tractor maker's first car and its V12 produced a very respectable 290 bhp.

driver Tony Rolt. The system had been tried in racing cars and found to be very successful, especially in wet conditions where the outstanding grip and traction overcame the penalty of extra weight. Jensen had tested the system in their older glass fibre bodied C-V8 model and decided to press ahead with a brand new car.

This new car used a chassis based very much on the C-V8 but the bodywork designed by Touring of Milan and built by Vignale was extremely attractive, the two-door coupé having a large amount of glass and good accommodation for the front seat passengers. The four wheel drive system consisted of a central differential mounted on the chassis, from which propellor shafts ran forward and rearward, the forward one running alongside the engine to drive an offset differential and thence to the front wheels by universally jointed shafts, while the rear one ran to the differential on the axle. The 6.2-litre (383 cu in) Chrysler engine was mated to a Chrysler Torqueflite automatic transmission.

This was not the end of technical sophisti-

A late version of the Lamborghini Miura, still one of the fastest production cars ever made.

cation because Jensen's Chief Engineer Kevin Beattie had also adopted the Dunlop Maxaret anti-lock braking system, which was designed to prevent the four disc brakes from locking on under panic braking manoeuvres.

Jensen announced the cars to the press in a demonstration at the Goodwood motor racing circuit, but journalists were puzzled at being first asked to drive the cars across some muddy grass then up steep grassy banks. The four wheel drive cars climbed these obstacles with ridiculous ease, and in fact the car could be stopped half way up the bank then restarted with no wheelspin or sliding backwards. Out on the racetrack the car cornered with remarkable agility for such a big machine and there was surprisingly little sign that all four wheels were driven, although the power steering masked any heaviness that might have been felt.

The extremely good-looking Maserati Ghibli had a 4.7-litre V8, but was otherwise mechanically similar to the Quattroporte. It was fast but did not handle well.

The big surprise came from the brakes; when attempting to lock all the wheels by braking with maximum pressure, the car would slow down rapidly and just as it seemed that the wheels would lock, the brake pedal would start pulsating and push the driver's foot backwards, easing off the brakes just sufficiently to prevent them from locking.

Technically the Jensen FF was a success, but commercially it was not. It cost very little less than a Rolls-Royce, had far less interior and luggage space and when it began to wear it had a lot of mechanical parts to go wrong. It was not much fun even for the wealthy to have to overhaul no less than three differentials when the transmission began to wear out.

The FF continued to be catalogued for a number of years but sales were small. Fortunately, Jensen also produced a less complicated version of the car called the Interceptor. This did not have the four wheel drive mechanism or the anti-lock braking and was consequently 30 per cent cheaper than the FF, which it resembled almost exactly, apart from the fact that it had only one air extractor grille behind the front wheels, while the FF had two.

The Interceptor was a fast car in its own right, being capable of 135 mph and having a 0 to 50 mph acceleration time of just 5 seconds. In 1972 there was even a hotted up version, the SP which had a highly tuned 7212cc (440 cu in) Chrysler engine, which had three Holley twin barrel downdraught carburettors (hence SP for six pack, or the six barrels of the carburettors), a compression ratio of 10:1 and a power output of 385 bhp at 4700 rpm. This gave the car a top speed of 150 mph, but the model did not sell very well as the market for the Jensen was with the businessman who needed silent, rapid transport without the fuss brought about by the use of a tuned engine.

The Sunbeam Tiger mated a 4.2-litre Ford V8 to the body of the Sunbeam Alpine with some interesting results.

Jensen went through a very bad time in the late 1960s and early 1970s as demand for their cars waned and eventually they succumbed to their problems, although, fortunately, they retained a service organisation to care for the cars that remained.

One of the most sensational road cars of the 1960s had its beginnings in Henry Ford II's ambition to win some of the major events in world motor racing. In 1962 he metaphorically tore up the agreement amongst American motor manufacturers not to take part in motor sport and threw his huge company's resources into a campaign that was to bring them victory at Indianapolis, victory in many rallies and victory in the best known racing event of all, the Le Mans 24 Hour race.

Henry Ford II had tried to buy Ferrari to make his path back into racing a little easier, but the old man had refused to sell and Ford privately vowed to beat Ferrari at his own game one day. He set up his own racing departments in America and Europe, hiring the best people to get into racing fast. In Britain Ford approached Eric Broadley,

owner of the Lola racing car factory, and offered to set him up in new premises if he would help them develop a new racing GT car based on his Lola GT which had made a promising debut in the 1963 Le Mans race.

The car was virtually redesigned in the next year and when it was announced it was renamed the Ford GT40, the number 40 being used simply because the car stood a mere 40 inches high. The car raced successfully, winning Le Mans by 1966, but Ford stood by a clause in the motor racing regulations for these 'prototype' cars that the cars should actually be prototypes of potential road cars. The road versions were built by Ford Advanced Vehicles at Slough in England, 31 of the Mk I model being built before it was superseded by the Mk III (the Mk II being a racing car) but only about seven of these were built before the programme was abandoned.

The Mk I road-going GT40 was very similar to the racing model in virtually every respect except creature comfort. The car had a very stiff chassis of monocoque construction welded up from sheet steel, with fairly high side tubs which held the fuel tanks. This precluded the use of normal doors so the tops of the doors were curved over to cut into the roof panel so that the driver and passenger could drop down into the car, rather than enter from the side. Front suspension was independent by double wishbones, coil springs, telescopic dampers and an anti-roll bar, while at the rear the independent layout was by double trailing arms, transverse top links and lower wishbones in conjunction with coil springs, telescopic dampers and an anti-roll bar. Braking was by Girling 11½-in diameter disc brakes on all four wheels, steering was by rack and pinion and fat little 15-in diameter tyres were mounted on alloy wheels.

The engine was mounted right behind the cockpit in the mid-engine position ahead of the gearbox. The unit chosen was the faithful cast iron 4.7-litre (289 cu in) V8 that was fitted to the

The Jensen FF brought four-wheel drive to 'ordinary' motoring. It used the Interceptor body with the Ferguson drive train. This is the Series II of 1970.

Mustang and many other Fords. In GT40 trim with four down-draught Weber 48IDA carburettors it gave 335 bhp at 6250 rpm. Power was transmitted through a twin plate Borg and Beck clutch to a German ZF 5 speed gearbox/final drive unit.

However, as a normal road car the GT40 had distinct limitations. It was difficult to enter and leave; the seating was less than luxurious; the noise level was high; the heat in the 'cockpit' was sometimes intense; there was no luggage room at all; and it was not exactly waterproof. Moreover, it had a heavy thirst for fuel, at some 15 miles per gallon, and its tank was commensurately large, with a capacity of well over 30 gallons.

However, although not the greatest road car of all time, the GT40 was immensely enjoyable to drive, and on the open road it came into its

element. It weighed a mere 2000 lb, and was naturally a very quick car indeed. It would accelerate up to its maximum revs in fifth gear with alarming ease. Moreover, it would reach 100 mph from a standstill in some 12 seconds – all on an ordinary old Ford iron engine which was hardly being extended.

Roadholding, steering and braking were outstanding, for, although they were up to racing standards, the car was very comfortable on bumpy roads, with none of the bone-shaking ride that is normally associated with racing cars.

Europe was in the forefront of the industrial revolution, but for various reasons some countries seemed to avoid joining in the race to industrialise. Spain was a prime example, possibly because of her remoteness at the southern end of Europe, hidden behind the barrier of the Pyrenees, but another country, Switzerland, developed her many natural attractions and seemed to be able to survive without heavy industry. There had never been a motor industry as such in Switzerland, the only make which had made any sort of mark being the Martini, which

The Pantera was developed from the Mangusta and was powered by a 5.7-litre V8 Ford engine, linked to a five-speed ZF transaxle.

went out of production in the 1930s.

After World War II, Switzerland became one of the most important markets in Europe as virtually all cars were imported and the Swiss, having been neutral during the war were free to import cars from any country they chose. The annual Geneva show has for many years been one of the most important in Europe.

It was against this background that a new Swiss marque was born in 1967. Peter Monteverdi had run a small garage in Basle, selling mostly BMWs for some years and he had built his own racing cars, called MBMs, until he was forced to retire after a bad crash. He then decided to build his own road car, named after himself. The new car was a luxury GT coupé using a chassis designed and built by Monteverdi but with virtually all the other components bought out. The chassis featured square section

steel side members with built up superstructures front and rear. Front suspension was by double wishbones in conjunction with coil springs and dampers while a de Dion axle was used at the rear, being located by a Watt linkage and parallel trailing arms. Steering was by the German ZF power assisted cam and peg unit and the brakes were Girling 12-in discs on the front wheels and 11.8-in at the rear, mounted inboard adjacent to the final drive unit.

Like so many other small European makers of quality cars Monteverdi used the big 7.2-litre (440 cu in) Chrysler 'hemi-head' V8 mated to the Torqueflite three speed automatic gearbox. Because the power output of this engine was 375 bhp the car was known as the 375S while a more highly tuned version which gave 400 bhp was called the 400SS.

Bodywork was designed and built by Fissore in Turin and the attractive lines brought a small but steady flow of wealthy drivers to Basle. Production was carried out in the workshops of Monteverdi's garage by the same mechanics who serviced customers BMWs, so production was

Ford's GT40 was a roadgoing replica of their Le Mans winner. The figure 40 came from the height of the car, a mere 40 inches.

limited to little more than one car a month.

Monteverdi introduced a slightly lengthened version called the 375L which sported a vestigial rear seat and in 1971 announced a new mid-engined car called the Hai (shark) which featured the Chrysler V8 mounted behind the cockpit. A five speed ZF gearbox was used and the de Dion rear axle was retained by kinking the de Dion tube over the transmission.

The bodywork was attractive but not as attractive as that of the Lamborghini Miura, which had a much more exotic specification. The Hai also suffered from a great deal of noise and heat in the cockpit as well as a difficult gear-change. With rather restricted space for both passengers and luggage and a price tag of £13 000 in 1971 it was not exactly in great demand and only three or four examples were made.

A four door car, the 375/4 was introduced in

1972 but this was also too heavy and too expensive to challenge the world's luxury makes. Perhaps the ultimate Monteverdi was the Berlinetta, based on the 375S two seater but fitted with the engine from the Hai which was alleged to give 450 bhp. A top speed of 180 mph was claimed but like many claims by Monteverdi it was optimistic and the car would only be persuaded up to 160 mph if a very long run was available.

Production of the Monteverdi proceeded at a trickle into the mid-1970s but the arrival of the oil crisis finally sealed the fate of the Basle manufacturer and the company quietly went back to servicing BMW's, although they did make a prototype of a smaller car powered by a BMW engine, which never went into production, and are currently building a four door version of the Range Rover.

The 1960s saw the arrival of one of the most revolutionary developments in the motoring world, the Wankel rotary engine. Felix Wankel had been working on rotary valves for many years and, in conjunction with Dr Froede of the NSU company, he developed the Wankel engine which eliminated the reciprocating motion of the internal combustion engine and replaced it with an epitrochoidal chamber (three overlapping chambers) containing a three sided rotor. The rotor spun on an eccentric shaft so that the tips of the rotors followed the shape of the chamber, three combustions taking place per rotation of the rotor. This engine was delightfully simple, having only three major moving parts against the dozens in a conventional engine, and friction was much reduced.

NSU fitted the engine first in a small sports car, the NSU Spider, but this was really only to evaluate the engine in service and they saved their major surprise until the Frankfurt Show of 1967 when they announced the Ro 80 model. Not only was the car fitted with the Wankel engine but it was a twin chamber rotary developing 115 bhp at 5500 rpm which was mated to a three speed gearbox having an automatic clutch, while drive

Monteverdi's 375 was styled by Fissore of Turin and sported the ubiquitous 7.2-litre Chrysler V8. This is the L version of 1970.

was taken to the front wheels. Front suspension was independent by McPherson struts and coil springs while the independent rear suspension used semi-trailing arms, coil springs and tele-scopic dampers. The whole thing was clothed in an attractive four door saloon body of tremend-ous grace which immediately captivated the motoring world, bringing forth a flood of 'Car of the Year' awards. The technical specification looked absolutely right for an advanced car of the 1960s and most observers felt this was the car that others would have to copy.

Sadly, cars have to work for their living, not sit on pedestals, and when the Ro 80 was put to work it showed some deficiencies. The rotor tip seals, which had worked well when driven by test

NSU brought the Wankel rotary engine to the public. This is the stylish Ro 80 which incorporated several innovations, but which, sadly, was rather fragile.

drivers who were sympathetic to the needs of the engine, began to wear at an alarming rate when put in the hands of the public. The engine was given a rev limit of 6500 rpm but so smooth did it feel that many drivers just went on revving way beyond its power peak. Although the official top speed was around 112 mph it would climb and climb on a suitable road, going up to 130 mph if the driver allowed it to. The design of the seals would not withstand this treatment and soon they wore, causing the engine to smoke a great deal and to consume oil. Finally, it would lose compression and refuse to start, necessitating a brand new engine. Since an unsympathetic driver could reduce an engine to this state in 20,000 miles, NSU's generous view of their warranty began to affect their finances, and although the problems were gradually overcome the damage had been done. The engine was also rather thirsty, and whereas an equivalent car would perhaps do between 26 and 30 mpg the Ro 80 would do from 19 to 24 mpg. This did not matter too much in the mid 1960s as fuel resources still appeared to be abundant, but by the mid 1970s the rotary was almost dead, partly because of its continuing unreliability, its high fuel consumption and the difficulty of modifying it to meet increasingly stringent pollution laws.

The Ro 80 was a fine car to drive, for it was smooth, silent and very fast. Once the driver became accustomed to the operation of the automatic clutch, gear changes could be made rapidly and quietly and the roadholding was the equal of virtually any other saloon car. Passengers appreciated the car as well, for the ride was soft yet well damped and the car was so well shaped that wind noise was kept to a minimum.

Unfortunately, the unreliability of the engine has forced many owners to seek alternative engines, the most popular being the Ford V4 2-litre unit taken from the Ford Consul range, although those seeking more performance have squeezed in the Ford V6 unit. It is possible to mate the engine to the existing transmission so the conversion is not horrifically expensive. Whilst this is a means of keeping the Ro 80 on the road the rather rough and noisy V4 destroys the original concept of the Ro 80.

With financial ruin staring them in the face in 1969, NSU were absorbed into Audi who were themselves immediately merged with VW, and although the Ro 80 carried on for a few years all confidence had gone and the name of NSU was dropped from the catalogues when the last Ro 80 was produced in 1978.

Although many other manufacturers took out licences to make the Wankel rotary engine under licence to power everything from lawn mowers to aircraft, from mopeds to ships the vast majority of them have fallen by the wayside and in the motoring field it has been left to Mazda with their rotary engined RX7 sports coupé to carry the flag for the rotary engine.

Despite the problems that were besetting the motor industry at the end of the decade Enzo Ferrari seemed intent on carrying on producing his exotic GT cars as if nothing had happened, although even he realised that some concession should be made to inflation and pollution problems, so in 1969 he came up with a new small sports coupé, the Dino 246GT.

The car was named Dino after his son Alfredino who died of leukaemia in 1956. There had already been several racing and sports Ferraris named after Dino, but the Dino 246 was intended to be a new marque name. Unfortunately, it did not work out that way as most buyers wanted the cachet of the Ferrari name. After all, who had ever heard of a Dino?

The car started in 1958 as the Dino 196, a sports racing car which had moderate success. This was mid-engined and powered by a V6 1984cc 225 bhp engine, which was followed by the Dino 206, another mid-engined car powered by a 1592cc version of the V6 developing 190 bhp at 9000 rpm. By 1967 the engine capacity had been increased to 1985cc and, with a cast iron block, was fitted in two front engined Fiat models.

By 1969 the engine had been developed into the 246GT with very over-square dimensions of 92.5 mm × 60 mm giving a capacity of 2418cc – hence the model name, 24 for the capacity and 6 for the number of cylinders. This neat little engine had twin overhead chain driven camshafts per bank and with three Weber 40DCNF-6 downdraught carburettors the engine developed 195 bhp at 7600 rpm.

The engine was mounted transversely across the rear of the car behind the cockpit and is in unit with the five speed all-synchromesh gearbox. The suspension is by wishbones and coil springs on all wheels with disc brakes on all wheels and steering is by rack and pinion.

The attractive coupé bodywork was much admired when it was introduced and although luggage space was at a premium it was regarded as a fit rival for the Porsche 911. Top speed was a very healthy 145 mph and because of its light

The Aston Martin DBS began life with the six-cylinder engine, as here in this 1970 car, but a new V8 was soon offered.

weight (just over a ton) it accelerated well and gave a fuel consumption of around 20 to 22 mpg.

The Dino was a delightful car to drive, with light steering, superb handling and all the right noises from the little V6 engine. The gearchange, with its positive external gate was a delight to use, as are most Ferrari gearboxes, and it could be thrown about in a most entertaining way. Unfortunately, the restricted access to the engine under its miniscule hatch and the general tight fit of the whole bodywork meant that servicing was quite a problem with the result that it was often neglected. A neglected Ferrari can give an awful lot of trouble!

Although the 1960s came to an end in an aura of gloom, with inflation and American safety and pollution regulations restricting development of the most interesting cars, there were still firms about which were prepared to make fine cars.

Ferrari's classic 246 Dino, surely one of the most elegant cars ever designed?

The 1971 Chevrolet Corvette Stingray still retained its fibre glass body but in a much more striking style than its predecessors.

THE 1970's

THE 1970S — END OF AN ERA

Looking back at 1970 from the safe haven of 1981 it might seem that knowledgeable people in the motor industry would be able to forecast what was going to happen in the decade ahead. The signs were all there; speed limits were being applied more and more rigidly all over the world. Some parts of Europe were still quite clear, but America had suffered an overall speed limit of around 55 mph for several years and Britain was about to discover what the 70 mph speed limit on Motorways was like.

In the USA the exhaust pollution regulations were biting really hard and companies were spending millions of dollars on getting their cars to meet the regulations, without improving their car's performance one iota. Indeed power outputs were dropping alarmingly, so much so that car weight and size had to come down to keep pace with the depressed performance. Whereas in 1968 the American V8 was being tuned to the limits in an effort to win sales, by 1970 the performance car was on the way out.

European manufacturers of exotic cars saw much of their market evaporate overnight, for although they could often modify their engines to meet American pollution regulations they would have had to redesign them completely to meet the safety laws, while fitting bumpers capable of withstanding a 5 mph crash would have ruined the appearance of most classic GT and sports cars. Many manufacturers simply decided that it was not worth the effort and withdrew from the American market, which for a number of them meant the end of the road, because the bulk of their sales were in the rich US market. Fortunately, others carried on and were able to re-enter America, but a lot of famous companies like Lamborghini, de Tomaso, Lotus and Aston Martin, to name but a few, had to withdraw either temporarily or permanently from the USA.

More problems for the motor car arose when the Arab-Israeli war suddenly awoke everyone to the fact that oil could be used as a political weapon and was also a finite resource. With the

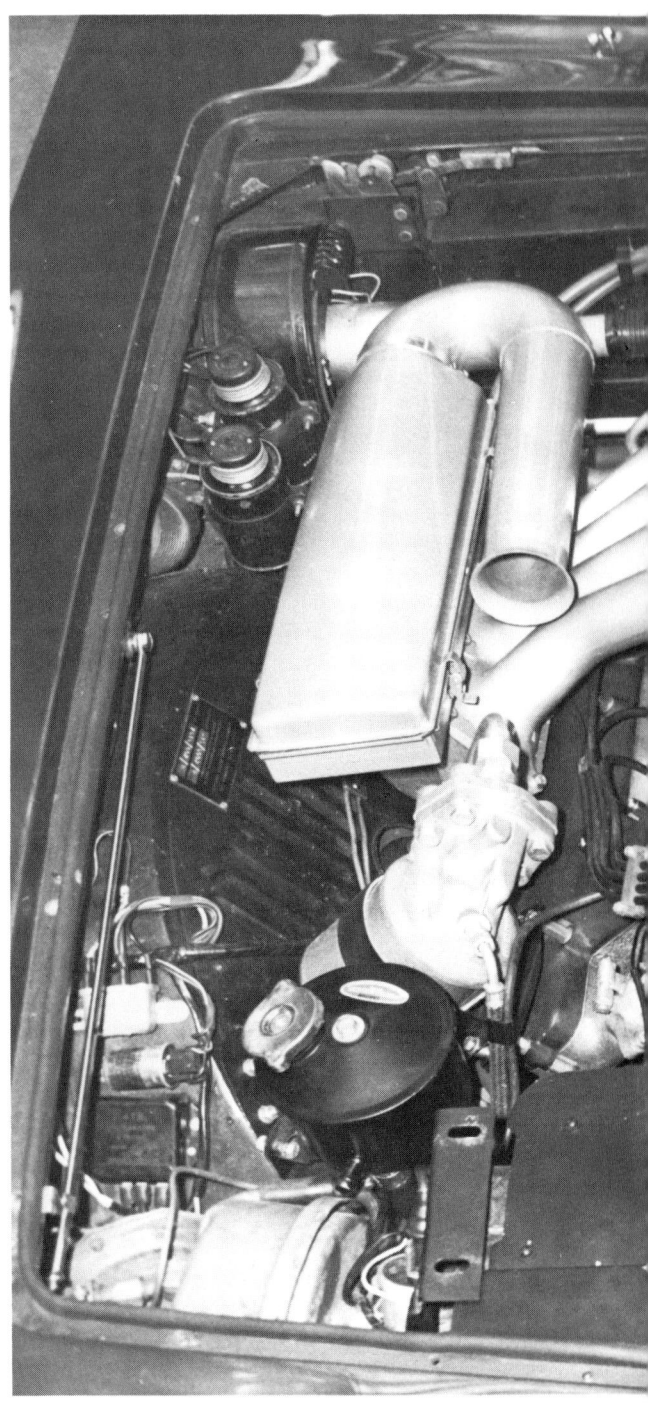

This is the superb four-cam V8, as fitted to the Aston Martin V8 and Lagonda models. It is shown here in its early fuel-injected form; Weber carburettors replaced this subsequently.

steep rise in oil prices that followed, the emphasis had to switch to fuel conservation, and although cars of the 1980s may not look too much different from their predecessors there is no doubt that the emphasis will swing more and more towards economy.

It is for this reason that the classic cars of the 1970s will be preserved by owners who do not want to lose the sort of performance which was possible in the carefree days before the various restrictions began to affect motoring. Already there is a ready market in the USA for high quality older cars which do not have to meet the strict laws which were brought into being in 1968, while a sort of cottage industry has built up in which clever mechanics modify exotic post 1968 cars to meet the regulations.

The number of collectable cars built in the 1970s has undeniably diminished in comparison with the 1960s and the monotony of the look-alike tin boxes made by the major manufacturers has focused enthusiasts attention on older cars. Many quality makes fell by the wayside and several famous names have struggled through the 1970s. Maserati were abandoned by Citröen and rescued by de Tomaso; Lamborghini went through two changes of ownership, a spell in the receivers hands, and are currently still struggling for survival; even Rolls-Royce went bankrupt, but were rescued; Jensen struggled hard against the problems posed by the American market but eventually succumbed; Abarth in Italy went out of business as far as car making was concerned; British Leyland dropped the Austin-Healey marque name; the Italian firm of ISO shut up shop; Lancia had to merge with Fiat to avoid bankruptcy; in Britain, Aston Martin under Sir David Brown had to give up the struggle, but were taken over by a property company who tried to keep the company viable and were rescued eventually by an Anglo-Canadian consortium, who in 1980 attempted a similar rescue act on MG, but failed to raise the necessary capital.

Aston Martin began the decade with a splendid looking new car, the DBS, with a body designed

The William Towns-designed Aston Martin Lagonda, a British four-door supercar.

Maserati's Bora was announced in 1971 and was the company's first mid-engined road car. Powered by a 4.7-litre V8 originally, the capacity had grown to 4.9 litres after a few years.

by William Towns. This big, sleek, low car was much better looking than the rather dumpy DB6 it replaced and was enthusiastically received by Aston Martin fanciers. The car featured a widened DB6 frame with the bodywork built up in aluminium on a tubular frame. In place of the rigid axle used on the DB6 a de Dion axle located by trailing arms and a Watt linkage were fitted. Front suspension retained the familiar wishbone and coil spring layout. An innovation was the use of Armstrong Selectaride dampers, which, as the name suggests, allowed the stiffness of the dampers to be varied while on the move.

Initially the car was fitted with the familiar straight-six twin overhead camshaft engine which was available in normal (282 bhp) or Vantage (325 bhp) trim, and although the latter gave the car a top speed of 145 mph and a 0–100 mph time of 18 seconds it was still not fast enough for the super-enthusiasts, so Aston Martin began work on converting their racing V8 engine into road-going form. This twin camshaft per bank engine had been designed for long distance sports car racing, but it had proved rather heavy and unreliable and the racing project was abandoned. But it was very successfully converted into a road engine and although Aston Martin declined to give power outputs, this 5340cc (325 cu in) engine was obviously very powerful as Aston Martin claimed a top speed of 161 mph, a standing start $\frac{1}{4}$ mile in 14 seconds and a 0–50 mph time of 4.5 seconds: all this from a 2 ton car!

I found the DBSV8 a difficult car to drive fast; it is heavy and the suspension is very firm for a luxury car, so it calls for quite a lot of effort to hold the car steady on bumpy roads. Its German ZF gearbox is not the most sophisticated unit and quick, quiet gearchanges are not easy to make. However, it is very fast in a straight line and makes all the right noises.

The latest owners of the Aston Martin Company not only improved the V8 when they took over (the DB, standing for David Brown had been dropped) they began design work on a luxury four seater which was given the name Lagonda, like so many luxury versions of Aston Martin models in days gone by. Mechanically, it was very similar to the V8 Aston, with virtually the same chassis layout and power train, but the wheelbase was increased by nearly a foot to 9 ft 6

in in order to make room for the four door, four seater bodywork.

The bodywork was the most sensational aspect of the car for it was very angular and flat sided with a very shallow nose, allowing room only for a vestigial radiator grille like a cut down Rolls-Royce radiator. The company had also tried to project themselves into the electronics age in a big way by eliminating conventional instrumentation and replacing it with a computer controlled electronic LED (light emitting diode) display system in which every piece of information about the performance of the car could be monitored. Many controls were actuated by touch-buttons which use the conductivity of a person's skin to complete their electrical circuit.

Unfortunately, the company paid the price of

In Italy the supercar manufacturers still managed to build their exotica against ever increasing odds and the three main manufacturers in this field, Ferrari, Maserati and Lamborghini were joined by a newcomer – de Tomaso. In reality, Alessandro de Tomaso was no newcomer as he had been driving racing cars in America and Europe for many years. Of Argentinian extraction, he married a wealthy heiress, Isobel Haskell, and they moved to Italy to build road and racing cars. For many years de Tomaso dabbled with weird designs, seemingly more interested in an abstruse technical challenge rather than actually getting a finished car on the road. He built a racing car with a cast magnesium bathtub shaped chassis which never raced and several other designs which were never finished. He built a backbone chassis coupé, the Vallelunga, powered by a Ford Cortina engine, but only a few were built. His first design to attract real attention and to go into serious production was the Mangusta (mongoose) which was a rear-engined coupé powered by a Shelby tuned 4.7-litre Ford V8 engine, tuned to give 305 bhp (SAE) at 6000 rpm. This car also had a backbone chassis built up from sheet steel and the all-independent suspension was by wishbone and coil spring.

A rather nice coupé body was designed by the Ghia works and de Tomaso claimed a top speed of 155 mph for the Mangusta. I was to find that it needed a brave man to drive at those speeds on anything but a wide, straight road, because over 60 per cent of the car's weight was behind the driver. I first drove the car near the de Tomaso factory in Modena and was at first quite pleasantly surprised by the lightness of the steering. It was only when I reached some interesting winding roads in a hilly district that I discovered why the steering was so light – the tail swung outwards viciously as soon as any power was applied, calling for continuous twirling of the steering wheel to keep the car on the right side of the road. This was quite fun to begin with but it became tiring after a while, and buyers obviously felt much as I did for sales were never very brisk.

Fortunately for de Tomaso, Ford of America took an interest in the car at this stage. They were still pursuing their high performance image and they offered to market the car in the USA and in

Introduced in 1972 as the fastest production car in the world, the Ferrari Berlinetta Boxer was actually no faster than its front-engined predecessor, the Daytona. This is the 5-litre 512BB of 1979.

many pioneers because the electronics gave endless trouble during testing, and deliveries were held up for many months. Eventually, the first car was delivered to the Marchioness of Tavistock on a trailer, as the electronics were still not working! The company has dropped many electronic components and production cars are now reaching customers who have the necessary £50 000 and are prepared to wait a couple of years for their car.

return put some money into the de Tomaso company as well as purchasing the Ghia company from him. Ford felt that the car needed many improvements and in the end the car was so changed that it was given a new name – Pantera (panther). Although the bodywork was the same general shape it had been cleaned up considerably and looked much sharper, while the standard of engineering on the chassis was much improved. The backbone chassis was superseded by an integral chassis/body unit and the engine was replaced by a 5763cc (351 cu in) Ford V8 mated to the same five speed gearbox. This engine gave 330 bhp (DIN) at 5400 rpm and endowed the car with a genuine 160 mph top speed. The Pantera handled much better than the Mangusta and it began to sell well all round the world. Unfortunately, the American safety regulations make it uneconomic to keep changing the car for the US market and exports had to stop, but by then de Tomaso was well established and he went on to build other versions of the car, such as the GTS, which had a 350 bhp engine and a claimed top speed of 174 mph. He also moved into the four door saloon market with the Deauville and a 2 + 2 coupé, the Longchamp. De Tomaso was established as a fully fledged manufacturer by the mid 1970s and he soon began to acquire other companies, taking over Maserati and the Innocenti factory, which made Minis under licence. He also acquired two Italian motor-cycle firms and put them back on their feet.

In 1971 Maserati announced an unusual road car for them, as prior to this new model, the Bora, they had stuck to front mounted engines. In the Bora they fitted their big 4719cc (288 cu in) V8 behind the driver, mated to a five speed trans-axle unit. The chassis was an integral unit with the all-independent suspension by wishbones and coil springs. The bodywork of this two seat coupé was rather bulbous and brutal; the roof line merged into an almost horizontal tail section and Maserati had to let glass panels into the tail side sections so that the driver could see to reverse the car.

The effect of driving the car was somewhat claustrophobic as the glass area was not very generous, but it could be argued that you do not buy a £9000 supercar to spend much time backing up with it. Certainly, when going forwards it was an impressive beast as it would cover the standing start ¼-mile in 14.5 seconds and although it would not quite reach the 174 mph that Maserati claimed from the 310 bhp engine it was fast enough for most drivers, although it consumed fuel at a prodigious rate.

With the Citroën takeover of Maserati, the French company introduced a smaller engined version, using a new Citroën-Maserati V6 engine of 2.9-litres (109 cu in) which gave 190 bhp in normal form and 220 bhp in the SS model.

The Bora's engine grew to 4.9-litres (309 cu in) and although power only increased to 320 bhp it was produced lower down the rev range, thus making the car more reliable and more tractable in traffic.

Maserati's great rivals in Modena, Ferrari, had, by and large, stuck to the front engined formula for their road cars, the small engined Dino range being brought out to counter the ever growing market for Porsches. However, in 1973 they introduced a new mid-engined car, the Berlinetta Boxer, which they claimed was the fastest production car in the world with a top speed of 188 mph. The car featured a tubular steel chassis with many welded steel panels, and suspension was independent all round with double wishbones and coil springs. Power came from a new horizontally opposed 12 cylinder engine of 4390cc (268 cu in), producing 380 bhp at 7500 rpm. The engine was mated to a five speed trans-axle unit, braking was by servo assisted discs and steering was, slightly surprisingly, by worm and roller.

The car was clothed in a body fairly similar to that of the Maserati Bora, but subtly more aerodynamic and better looking, as well as giving better visibility, because of the low height of the engine. Those few magazine testers brave enough to try to discover if the Boxer would do 188 mph found that it stopped well short of that velocity – mercifully perhaps. In fact it was no faster than the previous front engined Daytona model and Ferrari in some embarrassment increased the engine size to 4924cc (302 cu in) and raised the power output to 360 bhp at 7100 rpm. This model, the BB 512 was also claimed to do 188 mph but it would not do it either! Since there are now very few countries left in the world

where it is legal to attempt this sort of speed it is fairly academic anyway, but Ferrari were rather embarrassed over their failure to match their claims. They explained it by saying that they reached this speed with their pre-production prototypes but the cars were inadvertently fitted with an engine producing more power than the production engines.

Whatever the wrongs and rights of the BB it is a magnificent car in which to ride, although, like the Bora, the GT40 and Miura it is rather impractical.

Not to be outdone by lesser makes, Rolls-Royce rose Phoenix-like from the ashes of the 1971 receivership and introduced the new Corniche first, fitted with the choice of two door coupé or convertible bodies by Mulliner-Park Ward and then in 1974 astonished the world, and possibly themselves, by announcing the Camargue, a vaguely sporting car, from a company who had previously eschewed any attempt at a sporting vehicle. The car used the mechanical components from the Corniche in slightly modified form and clothed them with a body

The Pininfarina-styled Rolls-Royce Camargue of 1974 marked an attempt by the company to build a slightly sporting image into its products.

designed by the house of Pininfarina in Italy. This two-door coupé has more than a passing resemblance to that company's body design for the Fiat 130 coupé, but the Camargue is so well balanced and grand that it hardly matters. The familiar radiator contracted yet more to fit the lower contours of the Carmargue and it was flanked by the quadruple headlamps which had upset Rolls-Royce enthusiasts so many years before.

The familiar all-aluminium V8 engine of 6750cc (412 cu in) is again mated to the three-speed automatic gearbox, and as with all Rolls-Royces no power output figures are given, but it must be 'sufficient' because the car will reach a top speed of 118 mph and accelerate quite smartly as well. When it was announced in 1974 it was the most expensive car in the world at £29,250, but inflation helped to increase it to

£72,000 in five years, although this has done little to decrease the two year waiting list.

It is difficult to describe the sensations felt when driving a Camargue, for in truth it is a little disappointing in some respects. Naturally, the car is luxurious and the driver is greeted by the sumptuous smell of leather, while the walnut capped dashboard is as agreeable as ever. The car is quiet, too, but not perhaps as silent as one would expect, a fact commented on by American magazines who tested it against such cars as the Lincoln Continental and Cadillac and found that they were quieter. Perhaps the real difference is that in ten years time the Camargue will still be fairly quiet, while the 'Yank tanks' will be piled in some corner of a scrapyard.

The steering of the Camargue is terribly light, although it is geared only three and a quarter turns lock to lock, but the steering wheel seems eerily remote from the front wheels and the driver has little idea what is happening when he turns the wheel. The suspension, too, is very soft, which gives a lovely ride on smooth roads, but when the going gets bumpy the suspension travel is used up very quickly and it can bottom harshly.

As it weighs nearly three tons ready for the road the Camargue can hardly expect to have

sporting handling, and its progress is best described as stately. It is inevitable that the Camargue will be more at home rolling quietly down Park Lane or Fifth Avenue than hustling round country lanes, but one may wonder what sort of sports car the Rolls-Royce engineers could design if they had the chance.

Perhaps one of the most anachronistic cars still made is the Morgan. At a time when real vintage cars are in such short supply that firms like Panther, Excalibur, Felber and Stutz make replicas of old cars, the Morgan company from Malvern are still making the same vintage car they have always made.

That is not strictly true because the car has changed in many ways over the years but it still retains its separate chassis with Z-section side members, the curious sliding pillar front suspension and live axle mounted on semi-elliptic leaf springs – all of which the Morgan had more than 40 years ago. Naturally, there have been many detail changes, strengthened parts and so on but were a Morgan owner who died in the 1930s to

Straight out of the 1930s it may be, but the Morgan Plus 8 is extremely quick and very much in demand.

come back today he would have no difficulty in recognising the current Plus 8.

Morgan had used a variety of engines in their cars over the years including JAP and Matchless motorcycle engine, as well as Anzani, Coventry-Climax, Ford, Standard and Triumph units. The engines fitted to the four wheel Morgans had been four cylinder engines, but for the new Plus 8 Peter Morgan opted for the Rover 3.5 litre V8 engine, a unit which had been developed from the American Buick all-aluminium engine. Somehow the V8 was shoehorned in, aided by a small increase in chassis and body width, although I was amused to note when I drove an early production model that the cylindrical air cleaner atop the Rover engine had been 'persuaded' to fit under the bonnet by the simple expedient of hammering dents in the air cleaner!

With about 155 bhp available from the V8 engine the lightweight Morgan went like a scalded cat, reaching 100 mph from a standstill in 19 seconds and going on to a true top speed of 125 mph, although in truth it required some bravery to reach this speed on anything but a smooth road because the near solid suspension gives a very harsh ride and the car becomes airborne very easily.

I first drove the Plus 8 on a warm summer day when my wife and I spent a pleasant day zooming around the Vale of Evesham close to the Malvern factory, buying up all the fresh fruit in the area. It is a wonderful car for that sort of day, but on a damp February day in a Manchester traffic jam it must be purgatory. Like so many of the cramped, noisy, bouncy sports cars that the British have produced, the Morgan is either loved or loathed – there can be no half measures.

It is a tribute to the regard with which the Morgan is held by owners that there is a permanent two to three year waiting list for the few hundred cars built each year.

Perhaps the last word should go to a make which has done almost as much as any other in its short history to make motoring a true joy. The make is Lamborghini and the car which may well go down as the last great Supercar is the Countach.

The true successor to the Miura, the Countach is outrageously outlandish in almost every

Loosely based on the SS100 of the 1930s, Panther's J72 is one of a modern crop of replicas aimed at reviving some of the great lost names from the past.

respect. It is only 42 inches high, it is difficult to enter and leave, it is almost impossible to reverse, it has virtually no luggage space and it is horrifically expensive. Yet, many enthusiasts would cheerfully donate one of their limbs to have one of these beautiful cars sitting in their garage.

The basis of the Countach (pronounced Contash) is a tubular steel chassis frame with front suspension by double wishbones, coil springs, telescopic dampers and an anti-roll bar, while the independent rear suspension is by wishbones and trailing arms with coil springs, telescopic dampers and an anti-roll bar. Steering is by rack and pinion and braking is by $10\frac{1}{2}$-in servo assisted discs.

The motive power of the Countach is the familiar light alloy V12, four overhead camshaft unit with a capacity of 3995cc (240 cu in) which gives 375 bhp (DIN) at 8000 rpm using six Weber 45DCOE carburettors.

Unlike the Miura, the engine is mounted in the fore-and-aft position ahead of the five speed gearbox, thus giving a true mid-engine position at the expense of cockpit and luggage space.

The bodywork of the Countach is almost futuristic, reminiscent of the sort of styling studies that many manufacturers build to attract attention to themselves with no intention of putting them into production. With its almost straight-line sweep up from the air intake to the top of the screen, then the near horizontal line along the roof, the Countach is beautifully shaped to cleave its way through the air.

The one purpose of this car is to go as fast as possible, since it could hardly be called a sensible touring car. Lamborghini claim a top speed of 196 mph, which is very ambitious and very untrue, but even if it 'only' does 175 mph, that is pretty fast, and if you have just paid £50,000 for it then you are hardly likely to risk it by trying to go flat out.

With ever increasing legislation on safety, pollution and speed limits it seems that the days of the Supercar are numbered, and it may well be that the Countach will be the last of the high speed grand touring cars.

This pessimistic view may well be overtaken by events. Let us hope that science evolves a new fuel or a new power source to enable individual transport to remain practicable and to enable drivers to select a car to suit their needs, so that we do not have to look back on the 1970s as the 'Good old Days'.

INDEX